THE FIRE OF YOUR LIFE
A SOLITUDE SHARED

THE FIRE OF YOUR LIFE
A SOLITUDE SHARED

BY MAGGIE ROSS

WITH A FOREWORD BY
MADELEINE L'ENGLE

Paulist Press   New York/Ramsey

All psalms are taken from the
1979 Book of Common Prayer.

Unless otherwise indicated,
biblical quotations are from The Bible (Revised Standard Version).

The Publisher gratefully acknowledges
The Living Church for permission to reprint
"The Answer to Nicodemus," "Visions and Vision,"
"Intercession," and "All Hallows Eve."

Excerpts from the poems of Rainer Maria Rilke, translated by
J.B. Leishman, are reprinted by permission of The Hogarth Press, London.
The excerpt from *The Cocktail Party* by T.S. Eliot, © 1950 by T.S. Eliot,
renewed 1978 by Esme Valerie Eliot, is reprinted by permission of
Harcourt Brace Jovanovich, Inc., New York and Faber and Faber, London.
Material from *Descent Into Hell* by Charles Williams is reprinted by
permission of Wm. B. Eerdmans Publishing Co., Grand Rapids and
David Higham Associates Ltd., London. Excerpts from
The Book of Common Prayer are reprinted by permission of Seabury Press.

Library of Congress Catalog Card Number: 82-61420

ISBN: 0-8091-2513-7

Published by Paulist Press
545 Island Road, Ramsey, N.J. 07446

Printed and bound in the United States of America

Contents

Contents

Dedication

to my parents
natural and spiritual
whose manifesting of the
love of God
has brought me into
being

Merciful Father, who confound the wisdom of this world, but give understanding to the simple; so enflame our hearts with love for you, that we may never be ashamed to be fools for the sake of Christ.

Foreword

We are all hermits. No matter where we are, or what our particular calling, underneath we are hermits.

That is one of the things a hermit friend of mine reminds us of in her book, which recounts her experiences, and so also recounts ours. Or, the experience we would be having if we paused to be aware of our experience.

Maggie has chosen a special vocation, one which takes her far from the ordinary struggle of living life in over-crowded cities, affluent suburbs, and the failing technocracies of these late years of a war-wracked century. What can a hermit possibly have to say to all of us who are caught in the midst of the "madding crowd"?

She has much to say. "We are all, each one of us, a hermit. . . . In the end we know that we are a unique creation of God, and alone because of that uniqueness, and that this aloneness become solitude is the meeting place with God. This is true no matter how social and communal our exterior lives may be."

I am writing these words of love and appreciation for all that Maggie has to say, sitting in a chair in a hotel room in Indianapolis. Too many lectures have been thrust on me this spring. During these hours of solitude in an anonymous room, I, too, am a hermit. This is part of my calling, despite the fact that I am also a wife, mother, grandmother. When my children were little I had to grab my hermit's solitude wherever and whenever I could find it, walking the dogs around the house at night and seeing, in the clear country air, the multi-levels of stars, the glorious unlimited time-space continuum, in which I shared in the *isness* of creation. Maggie talks about this too, this *isness* which we are often too busy to remember. We need a hermit to point it out to us.

I need Maggie to remind me that "we are all wanderers, dependent on the love of God to sustain us in this transient world—transient not only because of our mortality, but also because we live in a culture of transience and change, change so rapid that it is almost impossible to understand what is being done to us by a technology run riot and a course of commitments that make our corporate suicide not only thinkable but probable."

I am writing this Foreword in a time of terrible world crisis. I need this particular hermit's basic affirmation that no matter what hideous folly man falls into, God can redeem it, because the wholeness of creation is God's, and the love of God is given to us with such overwhelming lavishness that "after the Eucharist we should genuflect to each other because we are all walking tabernacles."

Maggie is not a hermit because the world is evil and she must withdraw from it in order to save her soul. She is a hermit because all that God created is good, and this is her particular way of affirming this goodness. And she is not a hermit because of her own special spiritual virtue which sets her apart from the rest of the world. She is a hermit because it is her calling, one which I have watched her fight and reject and struggle against for many years. Now that she has succumbed to this difficult, extraordinary call, she writes, "My own failures . . . (are) too obvious for me to be anything but a sign of contradiction. God in Christ Jesus cancels all my condemnation and makes my darkness light. So it is for each of us." Amen.

She offers solid, realistic advice on fasting, on seeing and understanding our visions, on the differences between analysis and confession. She makes it clear that chastity is as important for the married as for the single, for those of us in the world as for the hermit. She clarifies many misconceptions about intercessory prayer. She makes many things possible, much joyous, almost nothing easy.

She writes out of her own hard-won experience, pragmatically. And she writes as a poet about that which cannot be expressed except in poetry. We see her encounter with the red bull through poetry, we feel the wild, electrical storm as poetry, we understand the casual death of a bird as poetry, for only through poetry can we accept the fact that we cause damage and death inadvertently even more than advertently, and that we cannot separate ourselves from the callous greed which caused the people of Minamata in Japan to die hideously of mercury poisoning.

She writes as Maggie, as a struggling human being turning fearfully away from God; she writes as one finally accepting the call and sharing with us all that she has learned in the struggle. And so, in the end, she is able to move through pain and death and share the glory:

"When we truly hear him, when we truly utter him in the silence of adoration, we participate in creation and the healing and transfiguring of creation. We utter him as we bear him, as our prayer becomes increasingly wordless and imageless; as we participate more deeply in his love we know that the kingdom of God truly is within us, that we, like John, are bearers of the light, lamps in the windows of God's house, fired with the oil of repentance, keeping us burning with him as we wait for him.

"Jesus, son of the living God, be borne in us today."

Even so, come, Lord Jesus.

Madeleine L'Engle

Introduction

My life has been a very ordinary life, from most points of view, and I am a very ordinary person. I have two parents who raised me in the ordinary way of things. We had the usual problems any family has, and the usual pleasures as well. I was raised to be a productive member of society as that is commonly understood; like everyone else without exception, created to love and adore God because he is.

Perhaps it is that awareness of being created to adore breaking through the ordinariness—rather, perhaps it is the awareness that being created to adore is itself the ordinary way into which we are all born—that is at the heart of so much of our disbelief. It simply can't be that ordinary. God's love simply has to express itself in more spectacular ways than the ordinary run of things, the particular mode of each of our ordinary lives by which we adore him, live out our yes.

The fire of God, the life of the Blessed Trinity, lies at the heart of all being, of every person, of you and of me. It is the source of the inframutability of energy, matter, Spirit, the coinherence of all the goodness of the universe in one eternal moment. It burns away the veil between life and death and enables us to share God's own life with one another and with those who have gone before.

Often our lives seem to be disconnected fragments: it is this loving fire that fuses the pattern, remains the constant; it is the love that undergirds. We can watch—if only we will—like a child looking through a kaleidoscope, transfixed by chips of glowing color falling into new geometries.

This fiery love, this burning life enfolds us within itself and all lives within itself, and within each of us. It is the clear, simple yet hidden vision that remains on the subliminal border of *gnosis:* impossible to conceptualize and talk about, yet we are impelled to try by the power of that gaze, concealed as it may be from ordinary consciousness. We know even as we attempt to communicate this love that only the vision itself and our following where it leads will satisfy the hunger it engenders.

Somewhere deep within us we have made the assent for the whole of our life, and struggle as we might, rebel, turn aside, there is no longer any real choice. Part of our thanksgiving on each return to its focus and flow is that the compelling beauty of this vision of love has once again overridden our mistaken path and falsely exercised freedom. God has recognized our deepest response, deepest surrender, and gently transmuted all of our turning away into this same yielding.

I could write, of course, more simply of goodness and joy, truth and beauty, and the embracing of death in the hope of resurrection, but so many of these words have lost their meaning through misuse or demythologizing that we have to evolve a new understanding of the individual journey each of us makes to the same end.

Thus there is nothing special about my life as a hermit: it is simply the way I live out my ordinariness, the way God has asked me, for reasons known only to him, to give my yes.

I have fought against this yes, gone entirely in the opposite direction, done everything I can to deny this summons, but he has always irresistibly brought me back. I've developed some flip answers to the question "Why are you a hermit?" not because I don't take the question seriously but because there is no possible answer that can communicate what is at work.

Sometimes I reply, "Because it takes a menace off the streets." (There is more truth than not in this reply.) Sometimes, "Because it's the only way I can embrace everyone at once." (Also truthful, but wholly inadequate.) Sometimes, "Because God has so preoccupied me with himself that no other response is possible." (True, but the problem is that this makes me sound special or singled-out. God calls us all to the same degree of union with himself.) Perhaps the most honest answer is, "I can't do anything else," and let the questioner understand that as may be.

Many writers speak of the things that are "said" by the life of silence and solitude, some of which are explored in these pages, too. One is that, in the end, for each one of us, there is only the mercy of God, and that this mercy can be the most painful thing in our lives to learn to live with, respond to, bear. "My yoke is easy, and my burden light"—but only to the degree that we cast off the burden of ego with which we are heavily laden, in order to be yoked and balmed by this fiery, purifying mercy.

Another insight made available to us by the hermit's life is that we are all, each one of us, a hermit; that in the end we know we are a unique creation of God, and alone because of that uniqueness, and that this alone-ness become solitude is the meeting place with God. This is true no matter how social and communal our exterior lives may be. It is within the interior solitude, the solitude and silence that many of us (including hermits) try to shut out with noise and activity of various sorts in order to evade that encounter, that we are called into truth and confrontation with mercy, that we are given what it is we have to give in our encounters with other people who in their own lives are engaged in the same searching.

A third message is that we are all wanderers, dependent on the love of God to sustain us in this transient world—transient not only because of our mortality, but also because we live in a culture of transience and change, change so rapid that it is almost impossible to understand what is being done to us by a technology run riot and a course of nuclear commitments that make our corporate suicide not only thinkable but probable. Perhaps the life of solitude, which lies at the heart of communal life, makes communal life possible, offers one alternative to blowing ourselves up: because true community, true life together whether in love relationships or formal monastic community can spring only from a solitude that is embraced by each.

Let me say, however, that I don't mean intentionally to convey any of these things with my life. I'm not in solitude to "say" anything; it's truly the only thing I can do. And by that I mean I'm miserable living any other way.

The reason for this is my own weakness as much as anything else, and one evidence for me of the power of the mercy of God is that he uses this very weakness for his own ends. Grace builds on nature, as the old slogan tells us.

There has been a lot of cult activity in our century. We seem to have an insatiable hunger for mystique, for instant satisfaction of the romantic, the visionary in ourselves, or of ourselves in terms of wishful thinking. This is no less true of the cults of film and rock stars as it is of suicide and outer-space cults, or the cults that thrive under the shelter of any organized religion.

It isn't so much that the cult, the mystique, focuses on the part instead of the whole, misses the mystery, appeals to the desire for dependence in us, to the shivery *frisson* of excitement to the exclusion of the holy or numinous; it's rather that a whole life gets sidetracked so that it misses its own self, its own point. We have often approached hermits in terms of mystique, and so have missed their own point.

Thomas Merton is perhaps the most prolific writer on solitude in this century, and he has some good things to say, though for whatever reasons his solitude was never as complete in an external way as he might have wished it, nor as it might have been. Nonetheless, although much mystique already enshrouds him, God has used that life to bring the idea alive before us as a counter-pole to our cultural thrust of a kind of hysterical togetherness and desire for repeated mass "experience" on which cults are built.

But solitude is its own *gnosis*, as it were, for each person, each individual. All the words about solitude can point to only one thing: the journey each must make, alone, to the meeting place with God who will send him or her out with his Word that will not return to him empty. There is no set way in which this is done, not even among hermits (or maybe especially not among hermits), any more than there are any two people alike. And it is, in any event, not so much a matter of doing as of being.

Although there are the words that make up this book, and the ideas that flow underneath the words, I have long since passed too many points of no return to be able to explain to anyone why I don't live as I might want, but rather as I must. My failures as a human being, much less as a Christian, much less within the mystique of the hermit some writers would have us believe, are too many, and too deep, and too obvious for me to be anything but a sign of contradiction. God in Christ Jesus cancels all my condemnation and makes my darkness light. So it is for each of us. There is nothing special about being a hermit externally as well as internally; it's simply what I must do by way of response.

The words themselves are very faint echoes of a single Word that has been spoken to me by those who have loved and taught me during my life, by creation itself, by the events of my life, and in the silence of still-prayer, which is at the core of each of us. This Word seeks to express itself in human speech, however feeble, to reassure us that the deeper we enter into the struggle with and search for God and our own solitude where he dwells, the more we come to know him who himself entered our struggle as man. There is no use talking of "progress"; one of the earliest lessons we learn is that we have to give up all geometries, all standards by which we measure ourselves against something. This is the insecurity into which we must enter: not to know, but to keep going.

It is often true of writers that they don't really understand what they have written until long after their paper or book has been published. This seems particularly true of poets and theologians and essayists. The essays in this book, however, are more so in the sense of verb than noun, more a movement than an explication, a thrust than an analysis. Where meanings are plural, all are meant, because it is always hoped that the Word behind the words will come through, give as many and wide meanings as possible, and as broad a perspective with each definition or description. Thus, apposite and paradoxical to the usual process, the writing seeks to give the most precise meaning by attempting to push into the most limitless.

Here, then, are fragments. Make of them what you will. If there is light for you, seek him of whose Word they are but poor reflections, splinters of a shattered mirror embedded in the flesh of a human heart that beats only because it is charged with the divine mercy and joy.

Ash Wednesday, 1982

DECEMBER

◆

The Answer to Nicodemus

The Answer to Nicodemus

In the beauty of holiness have I begotten you, like dew from the womb of the morning.

Abba, Father, fill our hearts with the quiet silence of that night on which your almighty Word leapt down out of your royal throne, and came to visit us in great humility; who lives and reigns with you and the Holy Spirit now and for ever. Amen.

We are entering the season of Advent, the time of expectancy, of hushed hearts and quiet waiting. And though many Christians generally don't make too much of her, it is the season of Mary.

For she is expectant, and when a woman approaches her term, there is about her a peculiar quality of great silence and quiet that communicates itself to the most casual passer-by, so that noises which are normally part of her environment become stilled. She moves about slowly, carefully, waiting for the first pangs of labor, or the breaking of waters that presage a new birth.

I felt this stillness most powerfully in my own life when I was ten years old, and my family was living in Washington, D.C. My mother, who was then forty, was about to give birth to my sister. It was as if the whole world were on tiptoe. And then one hot, humid June day, she went to the hospital and I was left home with a sitter. My older sister had been shipped off to summer camp. And I was very much alone.

The house, which was comfortable but not all that big, seemed to take on an aspect of hugeness, as if the walls were an illusion, and the silence grew tremendous as I waited for the return of my mother and the new brother or sister. Secretly I hoped that the baby would be a boy, because my father, in his good-natured chauvinism, had promised me an electric train if it were.

I never got that electric train, but it didn't matter because I was given something much more precious.

Forty is late to have a baby, and back in 1951 there was no specialty in obstetrics, as there is now, for mothers who are having children at the eleventh hour. As a result, or perhaps inevitably, my mother came home quite exhausted, and I was, in a sense, given my little sister to care for while my mother recovered.

I'm sure I had much less responsibility than I remember, but the deep bond formed with my sister during those first few months of her life remains to this day.

Her first years are the closest I've come to motherhood, unless you want to count the numerous stray teenagers who used to pass through my life, or deliveries at which I've assisted of dogs having puppies, sows having pigs, horses having foals and helping these surrogate progeny to some sort of useful independence.

The reason I detail all of this is that over the centuries, Mary has been so exalted by the Church as to become almost inaccessible to people like me who were not raised in an Anglican, Roman Catholic or Eastern Orthodox tradition. She is so surrounded by nonsense, so encrusted with cult, apologized for with such atrocious theology, that even the See of Rome sought to correct things a bit in its sensible decree from Vatican II.

Now if Jesus is God made man, I need his mother to be a very earthy woman, in the best sense of earthy and the best sense of woman, not some remote, impossibly slender creature, palely simpering in plaster. I need a madonna somewhat like the Flemish madonnas, with a peasant's face and a peasant's simplicity, who is not embarrassed to pull down her blouse to suckle her Child when he cries.

It is only from this base that I can begin to understand Mary as the exalted but quietly hidden Queen of Heaven, Queen of Saints, Mystical Rose, and all the other titles by which she is known. It is only from this base that I can read about the apparition of Our Lady of Guadalupe to Juan Diego and say, "Why not?" God uses the tools at hand and works through the uniqueness of culture, history, personality.

But to have come even this far in understanding the place of Mary in the Church and in my life has taken a long, long time.

Religion was rarely discussed when I was a child. My father came from a fundamentalist background, which he abandoned, and my maternal grandmother was deep into Christian Science, which was repugnant to my mother. And though there was never any real bigotry in our family, it was understood that while our Roman Catholic friends were very fine people, they were also possibly somewhat weak-minded when it came to matters of religion, and especially in their outlandish attitude toward the Virgin Mary.

So although I was drawn to her devotion at an early age, and in spite of the education of years, it is only in the last few that I've been able to say a Hail Mary without feeling guilty, or to use a rosary without being a little furtive.

In coming to terms with Mary, I had to start from scratch.

Recently there has been an explosion of studies in the long-neglected area of relationships between mothers and daughters, sisters and sisters. I won't detail them here. But unless you have been raised with the idea that Mary is, in a very real way, your mother, your attitude toward her, if you are a woman, tends to be slightly suspicious: Who is this woman and why should I pay attention to her? Why should I ask Mary to pray for me when I can pray to our Lord? How can I possibly identify with her life?

As time passed, I struggled with these questions while, very cautiously, allowing her a tiny corner in my consciousness, occasionally using the beads a friend gave me, half expecting to be struck by lightning at any moment.

Perhaps solitude has taught me more about Mary than anything else. Of all women, she was the most solitary. How could anyone possibly understand what happened to her? She must have experienced ridicule and disbelief. The very miracle of her life shut her off from the rest of women, except Elizabeth, whose conception of John by divine mercy was the closest she could come.

It was kind of God to give Mary that comfort. She had no other.

A more specific insight into the role of Mary occurred a few years ago on the Feast of Our Lady of Sorrows. If I had known the historical origins of this feast, it probably would have been yet another stumbling block, but being happily ignorant and somewhat literal, I celebrated the feast of a Lady who surely had a lot to weep about; and then, like an unexpected wave, the realization washed over me that here was the archetypal Mary, and my relationship to her was in the simple mystery that all women share, which is to weep over their men. And I believe that role stems as much from biology as from cultural conditioning. Women are haunted by a sense of loss from earliest childhood. Part of this may be rooted in the fact that the woman's reproductive system is itself hidden, and therefore a source of wonder and mystery.

And learning to deal with this inborn sense of loss is one of the hardest lessons a woman has to learn. It's significant, I think, that it was Luke, who was a physician and most likely to have an inkling of this aspect of women, who wrote of Mary that she pondered in her heart the unfathomable events surrounding her Son's life.

For although women, for whatever reason, seem more emotional, more prone to tears than men, they hide their deepest hurts—their own and those of their loved ones—in their hearts and never speak of them to anyone. And again, for whatever reason, this very secrecy seems to give women a kind of spiritual toughness and endurance they can draw on when they think they have reached their last reserves of strength.

One January, the sun was streaming at a flat winter angle through the east window of the hermitage, illuminating various items on the wall, including the little icon of Our Lady of Guadalupe that a Trappist monk had given me.

My journal for that day reads:

> When I picked up my rosary this morning—I was moved to do it by the sun on her icon—it was an act of pure faith and an uncomfortable one at that, like the candle that always burns

there. . . . But as I prayed, just letting the words run through my head, and the beads slip through my fingers, I realized that the angel was greeting not only her but also me . . . and that the bread made God and the God made Bread with which we live so intimately in the Eucharist was possible only because of her obedience, that the Sacrament is the earthly and tangible culmination of her saying "yes," that the rosary was my saying "yes," my prayer to participate in her yes in the fact of the Incarnation. . . .

I think that the Annunciation must have been an event of infinite and immense silence, for all the Gospel tells us of the conversation between them; wherever she was the walls or scenery pushed back, become transparent to reveal all that is, was, and will be, and then, within her.

And in thinking about that journal entry in the months since, it is by my baptism that I have said, "Be it unto me according to your Word," to bear that Word by the power of the Holy Spirit, and to bring him to fruition in my life. It's difficult to describe this experience of understanding, which may seem terribly obvious, but it shook me to the heart.

I took another step toward understanding Jesus' mother when I visited a Cistercian abbey. Just before I went there, we had the story of Nicodemus as the Gospel at Mass, and in the text we used, Nicodemus' question in response to Jesus' telling him he would have to be born over again was translated, "How shall this be?"

And immediately echoed in my head Mary's "How shall this be?" and Zechariah's "How shall this be?" and Abraham's laughter over God's preposterous proposal that he, at the age of one hundred, and Sarah in her nineties, could yet have a son.

But the significance of these echoes didn't really become apparent until I was complaining to the monks—who are most patient with me—about my problems with Mary, that no matter how hard I tried to understand, most of what has been written about her in the past seems as specious now as always. In response, they pointed to their own Cistercian spirituality, where Mary is not only the ideal model for the monk in her silence and hiddenness, but where the monk also is taken into her to be born with Christ.

Suddenly it all seemed to make sense, though I still can't articulate it very well. This is the answer to Nicodemus: that in order to bear the Word, to enter the Kingdom, we must indeed be born from the Spirit, not for the second time in the womb of our natural mothers, but continuously in the love of the Mother of God that brought forth her Son, and at the same time, like her, to bear him as well.

Mary, then, is my mother in this second birth, just as she is Nicodemus' mother.

That this is a paradox my heart is not yet big enough to encompass I readily admit. I still feel uneasy about Mary sometimes; there is still the flickering suspicion that perhaps I, too, am weak-minded. But, if nothing else, Mary has taught me to say yes: as Abraham and Sarah said yes, as Elizabeth and Zechariah said yes, as Jesus said yes to the cup that did not pass from him.

And each time that cup is passed to me at the Eucharist, because he has called me to wish to make that same response, I look into its depths beyond the dark wine shimmering gold and, trembling, I say, "Yes."

Visions and Vision

O God, by the leading of a star you manifested your only Son to the peoples of the earth: Lead us, who know you now by faith, to your presence, where we may see your glory face to face; through Jesus Christ our Lord, who lives and reigns with you and the Holy Spirit, one God, now and for ever. Amen.
— Collect for the Epiphany,
1979 Book of Common Prayer

Flying at 37,000 feet in a 747 jet is an experience unique to the latter part of our technological century.

The urge to escape the bond of gravity, however, is as old as man, whether breaking out of the physical realm, or spiritual, or from somberness into laughter, which are all aspects of the same desire.

And for me, it is summed up in the fall and spring when the migration of wild geese occurs, great flocks winging overhead, waking me in the night, or pulling me from my work in the early morning as they begin the day's journey, rising from nearby reedbeds and flapping heavily until they catch the updrafts of the rapidly lightening dawn.

Their cries call to me, evoking a longing, a homesickness, a tugging at my heart that often increases in intensity until I, too, flap my would-be wings, exultantly with them at first, then, slowing, and, a little embarrassed, sadly stopping because it is not given to me to join them.

But one can always hope.

The view from a 747 is higher than a goose enjoys, and the aircraft itself is very beautiful. The cabin is built on a continuous curve, and the broad wing has a reverse angle two-thirds of the way out that gives it a lovely sweep, leading your eye into infinity.

My last flight west to east was an advertising executive's dream: we took off in perfect weather, the engines' rumble calling in their own way to my earthbound yearning to be free, and, as the plane rolled down the runway, there was the mounting excitement that, feathers or no, we were going to *fly*, and then the intense pleasure of the behemoth's gently lifting off and becoming airborne.

Early snow had covered the western mountains and Great Plains, and as we flew past the sun, past the morning and noon toward dusk and darkness, clouds began to gather beneath us until, in the evening glow of our foreshortened day, the silver expanse of wing with its two cavernous engine pods pointed to fantastic shapes rising rose and mauve and gold over the horizon, and visions and hopes beyond speech.

We who are, by our biology, earthbound tend to study life from the point of view of microcosm, and from this intuit the macrocosm. But 747's help us a little to see, for once, our earth as a macrocosm that is really a microcosm of the universe.

The mystics find the universe, seen and unseen, in hazelnuts, grains of sand, and wild flowers. And their visions communicate to us a vision, a perspective, that widens the lens of our hearts, enabling us to glimpse through theirs a depth of field we had not dreamed existed.

Yet, these days, visions have fallen into disrepute. When we hear of someone having a vision, we tend outwardly to sneer with our empirical selves, a reaction that is more than a little fear of being laughed at for our credulity, and, inwardly, in our intuitive selves, the green-eyed serpent, Envy, twists and writhes and enjoys his Eden-born havoc.

For this split in us is diabolical: it is one of the most poignant results of the Fall, perfectly described in the allegory of Adam and Eve, who were not content with the direct perception of God and his creation, but wanted something more: the empirical knowledge that could and would, quite literally, put God to the test. This is our inheritance from our first parents, redeemed only in part by the vantage point from 747's and other mechanical imitations of wild geese.

But our curiosity about the lore of visions persists, and now psychology supposedly has given us a whole natural history which far surpasses Adolphe Tanquerey's succinct summary of three types of visions in his nineteenth century book *The Spiritual Life:* apparitions, imaginative visions, and intellectual visions. Thus by supplying us with a surfeit of descriptive jargon, these psychological empiricists encourage us to dismiss all visions as visualizations, self-hypnosis, hallucinations, hysteria, neurosis, psychosis, auditory dysfunction, indigestion, or the DT's.

The Church's own history of mania for classification and so-called other-worldliness occasionally has slipped into Manicheanism and Gnosticism in its denial of the goodness of *all* of creation, and implied that visions are secret knowledge imparted to the select few. This attitude has added to our discomfort with visions, so that we tend to think of them as not occurring outside certain rigid categories that are impossibly foreign to our age and experience, or, at the other extreme, as manifesting themselves in patently silly ways such as Bernini's sentimental marble extravaganza of St. Teresa in ecstasy.

But visions are the stuff of ordinary life, and without them we would long ago have yielded to despair. Because we do not often have them in the modes described by Tanquerey's tidy system, we tend not only *not* to recognize them as such, but also to miss the subtle direction God gives us in our lives and in our hearts' response which the perception of his overwhelming love elicits.

Visions such as Tanquerey describes still do occur. I heard, for example, of a lady who had an intense experience of the Passion of Christ in all three ways simultaneously while washing the dishes, and, characteristically, this lady, who happens to be a friend of mine, went right on washing the dishes through the whole thing. I'm sure she has never read Tanquerey, but the description, even second-hand, was classic.

Our visions are usually more indistinct, more oblique. We tend to think of them in the amorphous category of "ideas" or "ideals." The 747 began as an idea. The United Nations is both an idea and an ideal. The religious life is an ideal.

At year's end we are suspended in that unsettling period marking the end of one twelve-month cycle and the beginning of another in that sequence of convenience we call time. The sun has already begun its new round. Humans are a little behind, as usual, and while the sun knows its charted course, we use these days to do a little adding up: of our income taxes, our failures, our sins, and our successes, all in the light of projected ideas and ideals we had twelve months ago.

The result of this numerical and spiritual mathematics evokes mixed reactions: some of us will celebrate, some of us will weep; some of us will go to bed early, knowing that on January 1 we will still have with us the horrors of whole nations starving, torture in political prisons, nuclear insanity, and the rape of the earth and of our own souls. Some of us, having run out of ideals, having denied our visions, will commit suicide.

The word "vision" has become almost a dirty word in our technical religious lingo, and this is a tragedy. Paradoxically, when we speak in secular language it isn't so bad. We say, for example, of someone with new ideas, "He has a real vision." Or, listen to Celia in T. S. Eliot's play, *The Cocktail Party,* as she tries to describe to Reilly, a guardian angel posing as a psychiatrist, the motivating power of her life:

It's not that I'm afraid of being hurt again:
Nothing again can either hurt or heal.
I have thought at moments that the ecstasy is real
Although those who experience it may have no reality.
For what happened is remembered like a dream
In which one is exalted by intensity of loving
In the spirit, a vibration of delight
Without desire, for desire is fulfilled
In the delight of loving. A state one does not know
When awake. But what, or whom I loved,
Or what in me was loving, I do not know.
And if that is all meaningless, I want to be cured
Of craving for something I cannot find
And the shame of never finding it. . . .

You see, I think I really had a vision of something
Though I don't know what it is. I don't want to forget it.
I want to live with it. I could do without everything,
Put up with anything, if I might cherish it. . . .

While it may not be given to us, like Celia, to follow our visions to the end of being crucified on an anthill, we all *do* have
visions, every one of us, each according to his or her own nature. They are the deep, driving forces in our lives, and can be
evil as well as holy. And although we may on occasion have visions that resemble classical descriptions, our visions are, for the
most part, not seen even with our own inward eyes; they lie too
deep in us for that. To bring ourselves to an awareness of these
visions takes hard work, struggle, an unflinching examination of
self, the kind of objectivity that embraces pain and finds
Truth—yes, and even the Passion of Christ—at the kitchen sink.
It does not come about by chemical shortcircuiting of our physiology, or a casual gourmet pilfering of another culture's holiness.

A priest recently told me that the four things he cherishes
most in life, not in any particular order, are: being with his wife,
fathering his kids from diapers to adulthood, celebrating the Eucharist, and preaching. "I'm *always* preparing sermons in the
back of my mind," he told me. And there is no doubt at all that,
for the most part, when this man opens his mouth in the pulpit,
what comes out is extraordinary.

He told me, laughing, that someone he hadn't seen for a
while heard him preach one day, and afterward came up and
hesitantly asked if something unusual in the way of a conversion
experience had happened in his life. And my friend's reply was,
no, he was the same old sinful person, but he knew that when he
preached something else took over.

I believe that this priest's experience is common to us all in
the humble, ordinary stuff of our individual lives. When he is
sermonizing in the back of his mind, he is, in fact, not only trying to communicate, to make manifest, the vision of God which
he sees with and continually refers to in his heart, but also is engaged in worship, in adoration.

So too with each one of us. This vision of God, though we may not have recognized it as such, these visions of God give us the ability to know, even when we don't know, the direction of our lives. We thus have something in common with the wild geese and 747's that continue on through clouds and night, for, as Thomas Merton confided in a candid moment, "In the end, we're all flying blind."

But within this very blindness lies the perspective, the hope that keeps us from being overcome at year's end, that helps us face the ongoing holocausts, gulags, and daily petty cruelties to one another. It is the knowledge of our hearts of our forgiveness, that though blind we are yet given sight that beyond crucifixion is resurrection, that deep within us, calling us beyond conscious knowledge is the constant, loving look at the Father, which is Christ praying in us, and which oblique vision leads us to desire him with a love that can come only from him, and to grow in the purity of heart that, as we have been promised by Jesus our Lord, will bring us to see him face to Face.

What time-besotted earth, lurching among
the planets sees God's sense in revolutions?
Time-turnings in men's souls are never wrung
from safety into painless evolutions.
Not often have tangential lives become
one spiraled helix. Early on, mistrust,
like some fell Pegasus from fathers', sons'
own mingled blood springs. Ashes ground to dust.
Stunned by hatred, famine, pestilence,
a night of sense and soul, the old world reels
toward death: the young impelled to violence,
the agèd, fear. And angels break the seals.

Energy is made of rotting mass
times measured light. And man's forgivenness.

JANUARY

◆

Epiphany Penance

Epiphany Penance

Ho! Loser of Sins, bursting with absolution and Annie Dillard I've just tramped back from the woods, feet soaked, pant legs rolled up.

Springs flooding, streams springing from every where. Her soul and yours and mine riot through our solitary meadows crying Holy! and being burned, consumed. That's her line and she says it better, and she won't care.

And what about those three old kings? Kings, when the shekinah pervades like sin did and I throw back my head and exult?

One was a worshipper, an incense bearer. Me too. My clothes smell of incense from this morning. So do my hands. Incense, onions and wet leaves (the onions were in the chicken soup last night).

Oh, but I'm not staid! Not marching solemnly down church aisles or even clutching a camel. Like smoke, like the resins on the coals, I pop and explode and riot toward the roof and the cherubs sneeze and the ass brays and Mary laughs at my boisterousness and burning, and the Child names my secret name and is burning too, burning all of me that is not him, and he is not consumed.

Do you know about particles? They aren't. Matter is a mutable event, they say. Particles aren't points. They happen. There is no thing but interconnections in a cosmic dance of crazy mathematicians and the love of God.

Ah, father, Joseph, you are bewildered, caught—what of these caperings? What of your Vine? I am a whole nation of vines. We explode with bud-break in the spring, whirl, stamp and sing through summer and then, with him, go down to silence. We are crushed and pressed and poured in the cup he hands us.

Hey, Father. One of those kings was a priest. The myrrh-bearer. You are a nation of priests. You anoint me for my death, and I hear the groan in your soul—you can't fool me—when I touch his garment and you bring me back from the Pit.

Your sins are lost too: I yank them from you, laughing, when for one moment you take away from me all that is not him and he reaches through me. Oh, it's not Official. But I brought a gift to him, too.

And who is that third one, the gold-bearer? Maybe he's my father. Maybe he's your father. Maybe he's all the fathers who were greedy for their children's sakes, or greedy in the guise of their children's sakes.

Maybe that king's all the bitter, hollow husks, taking him gifts: their power and depression, and their lust, rejoicing in helplessness and nothing.

Days like these I wince at the Fraction and drink from the Cup, knowing each time I look into it I am asked and each time, trembling, I say yes, sometimes dreading, sometimes exploding, sometimes naught-ed by stillness in his center. And there we all are: you and Bonnie and the stray cat and me and the seven dwarfs (my ma ain't got no respect) and we're all up there transfigured with Moses and Elijah, and can't believe it, and neither can Booneville, which is there too.

And you know what?

The beginning and the end we can know now seem like, are like, are, darkness and nothing. Light and nothing—they are alike to him, we sing. And in that mutable event he creates, and even in getting there local or express, he ladles the molten stuff through us, finding holes in our tough webs, and, absolved, pours through the whole Bessemer converter, sparks crackling infinitely everywhere.

FEBRUARY

◆

Fast of Love

Fast of Love

Kind Maker of the world, O hear
The fervent prayer, with many a tear
Poured forth by all the penitents
Who keep this holy fast of Lent!
        The Hymnal, 1940, #56

Prayer and fasting. Fasting and prayer. The two are inseparably linked in every religion where there is the desire for God or entrance into the holy.

These days when there seems to be a reviving interest in prayer, fasting still has a bad name: it is unhealthy, destructive, masochistic. And yet, Jesus teaches us that the two are one, not only by his example of the forty days spent in the wilderness wrestling with evil and himself but also in his instruction to his disciples that certain problems can be dealt with only by prayer and fasting.

There is no question that fasting and its meaning have been distorted, abused, and caricatured until each Lent we experience what is left of our misunderstanding of this useful tool in a mild attack of conscience and the "give ups," rather like having an annual case of the flu. This is often accompanied by lugubrious interior sighs, which soon deteriorate into ennui, and finally expire into total indifference.

While the spectre of misuse of fasting by our self-destructive tendencies is very real, expressed, for example, in the lethal disease *anorexia nervosa,* which seems on the increase in our pressured times, or by those unbalanced in other ways, most of us can use fasting for what it really is: a means to an end, a re-

33

sponse of love to the God who first loved us, and an outpouring of this love to our neighbors.

First of all, fasting is not confined to restricting our intake of food. Fasting is not a diet any more than solitude is the same as living alone. Any time we say "no" to ourselves we fast, whether in a sudden surge of resolve to stop being seduced by a particularly fashionable act of immorality, or, at the opposite end of the spectrum, to give up a good option in order to make ourselves available for something of even greater value.

In this sense, prayer *is* fasting: when we pray, consciously or unconsciously, we make room for Christ's activity in us. In conscious still-prayer we gently eliminate everything else in our lives: activities, thoughts, distractions. We are saying no to ourselves in order to say yes to God, so that he can have his way with us; we are gaining control of our desires so that in the moment when he comes in his desire to kindle us into flame, we will be able to lose control, to yield entirely to him, and not run in terror in the opposite direction.

In this largest sense we can also say that fasting, rightly understood, is prayer, the famous "practice of the presence of God," or, to adapt the Buddhist concept of mindfulness, fasting is heartfulness, an opening of our hearts to be full of, aware of, God at every moment in our deepest being.

In this way we can understand the phrase from Psalm 51, "a broken and contrite heart," as a heart with clear knowledge of just who we really are in the light of the unbearable love of God and our intense desire for him, the yearning to increase our capacity for his love to enflame and pour through us. The pain is born of the humiliation of acknowledging the persistence and specific petty nastiness of our sins, which is a lot harder for most of us to face than the idea of cosmic evil.

Fasting is a response of love, and any other motivation perverts its meaning and becomes an abuse of the creation God has made to delight in. *Fasting is anything but self-punishment,* and any idea that we can make up for our wickedness is futile, as the Psalmist knows only too well: "We can never ransom ourselves, or deliver to God the price of our life; for the ransom of our life is so great, that we should never have enough to pay it."

Who are we to presume to punish what God has forgiven at the price of his own death? The wrath of God is his relentless and inescapable love for us.

Simply put, fasting can remind us of our longing for an unceasing conscious and unconscious focus on God, which is our whole lives' adoration.

Fasting, in its narrower and more usually understood sense in relationship to quantity of food, is an art in itself, but in no way replaces or obscures this larger perspective.

There are people who should not fast, in this more limited sense of fasting: the elderly, the sick. There are people whose metabolisms are brittle enough to make fasting in any way a bizarre experience. And excursions into exotic altered states of consciousness are definitely *not* the purpose of Christian fasting.

For these people, the inability to fast is itself the fasting, a humble submission to the will of God expressed in one's own unique physiology.

For the rest of us, fasting can take many forms: abstaining from certain foods such as meat; postponing the first meal of the day (an old desert practice); reducing the quantity of food; or, for extraordinary reasons, a total abstention from food *for short periods of time*—three or four days. There is no "right" standard of fasting except the impulse of a loving heart, which is God's doing.

It is now widely recognized by even the most austere monastic communities that each person must discover for himself by careful experimentation what is the most profitable way to fast. Often this requires a certain amount of ingenuity and improvisation, and inevitably in the process of observing our own reactions we become increasingly amused at the silly responses and phony excuses we manage to come up with.

This self-discovery is in itself a valuable result of fasting because it keeps us from taking ourselves too seriously, demolishes a secret smugness about our incipient holiness—only God is holy—and gives us a sense of *eutrapelia*, or entering into play with God, as Hugo Rahner has described in *Man at Play*. This attitude in no way detracts from the gravity of what we do, but enables us to do it with a light step, and with grace.

How do we know when to fast? Beyond the times suggested by the Church, and even at those seasons, it is a matter of listening to and with our hearts for the movement of love, which itself is a divine gift. This can occur as a sudden realization that we have forgotten God, or taken him for granted, a reawakening of our hunger to seek his Face that leads us into fasting, into the wilderness.

It can come with an appreciation for the goodness of creation so intense that we must go beyond the gift to the Giver.

Or the summons may come in a different way, an awareness of and desire to allow the love of God to pour through us on those who fast involuntarily in whatever mode, not only those who are starving, but also those who are deprived of the richness of life as we experience it: prisoners, hostages, invalids.

The idea of intercessory prayer as sharing our being with and for—in both senses of for: on behalf of and instead of—others is manifested, incarnated, by fasting in this context. An example of this is a person undergoing surgery who is deprived of all the normal functions of life including breathing, and the desire on the part of the one who prays and fasts to participate in that person's deprivation in the unknowable way that is infinitely beyond what we can ask or imagine.

But, and this must be stressed, this sort of fasting is *by invitation*, a definite call from God to undertake this work, and even if we are not invited to fast as we might expect or want, the practice of listening with the heart makes us ever more aware of the God whose life we wish to share, and surrender to him—fast from—our stereotypes of how the universe ought to work, and our role in it.

As with everything else in life, fasting has its particular techniques and pitfalls. The best way to approach fasting is not to make an issue out of it. Beyond the initial awkwardness that is part of anything new in our lives, and is best handled by patience with oneself, knowing that this preliminary self-consciousness will pass, fasting soon becomes part of the rhythm of ordinary life. Our Lord gives us specific instruction here: "When you fast do not put on a gloomy look as the hypocrites do: they pull long faces to let men know they are fasting. I tell you solemnly, they have had their reward. But when you fast, put oil on your head and wash your face, so that no one will know you are fasting except your Father who sees all that is done in secret, and your Father who sees all that is done in secret will reward you."

Sometimes we get an uncomfortable feeling that perhaps what Jesus is suggesting is a kind of reverse hypocrisy, an artificial cheeriness that sets our teeth on edge. But what he is referring to lies deeper than this: it is the sense of prayer without ceasing, of the self-forgetfulness that comes when fasting is part of the ordinary cycle of life over a long period of time, when fasting has become autonomic, though not unthinking. We become surprised by the joy and wonder and freedom of self-mastery *as a gift*, and not as a source of pride, which is the most dangerous and insidious trap in fasting or any other form of asceticism.

There are practical aspects to fasting, which have been spelled out in countless books on subjects as diverse as beauty culture and the occult. As we learn to fast, we discover our own particular methods and perils. We learn to make adjustments for our own physical needs. Some people require more bulk than others, for example. In general, nutritional research indicates that it is a good idea for the basic balance to be struck over a period of a week to a month, depending on the nutritionist you talk to and the particular individual physiology.

If we get beneath the encrustation of centuries, and allow for hagiography as an art form, the tourist desire to exaggerate, and the lunatic fringe, we can learn a lot about fasting from the sayings of the desert fathers.

Far from self-abuse, the desert fathers were well aware of the need for self-conservation in their extreme environment. Their basic diet consisted of a whole grain bread, dates, nuts, and vegetables. They gradually adjusted food and liquid intake until each discovered his or her (there were desert mothers, too) optimal balance. There is a touching story in the writings of Dorotheos of Gaza describing the tenderness with which he taught a young novice to fast over a period of years, weaning him gradually from old habits, and creating an atmosphere in which the common sense vital to growth into God could develop.

And common sense is the key to fasting. It is folly to fast when under any kind of strain. It is folly to fast if it makes you dizzy: drink some fruit juice. Don't fast if you have to drive or operate complicated machinery. Each of us has to discover these do's and don'ts by the examination of the obvious, but what is not often obvious is our pride, which can prompt us to do foolhardy things.

If fasting becomes an endurance contest, or develops into any other kind of competitiveness with ourselves or others, quit. It is much better to face the embarrassment of our pride than to continue. We can always begin again, a little wiser about ourselves.

On the other hand, there may be some tension when a person begins to fast, before fasting has become an ordinary element in the day, or in one's life. Laughter helps, and simply going about one's business. But continuing tension can also be a warning that we are too tired to fast, or that the timing, or perception of the invitation to fast, is awry. In learning to fast we must learn to make some very subtle distinctions.

Some people experience a surge of energy on the second or third day of a fast. There seems to be a physiological basis for this, as a great proportion of our energy is tied into digestion. Fasting can make us more alert, open our eyes to see God's hand in the world about us in a new way, and thus becomes an act of worship, joy, awe, wonder, and praise. We must never lose sight of the principal reason for fasting: to increase our awareness of and capacity for the God who is love.

Doing violence to oneself in any way is never part of prayer and fasting. Impatience, anger, sudden shifts of any sort are destructive. This applies equally in the physical realm as in the spiritual/psychological. It isn't a good idea to eat a lot the day before a fast. Go into it gently. It's a good idea to eliminate caffeine a couple of days ahead: some people get headaches from caffeine withdrawal on an empty stomach. Hot baths when fasting make some people jumpy. A fast should end with several small meals, beginning with juice and fruit, not with a celebratory binge.

Sometimes we may forget that we are fasting and break our promise; that is ordinary and human, and we should simply begin again when the time seems right.

It is often very valuable—indeed for many of us indispensable—to have help in learning how to fast from a friend who knows us well, an adept, or a director. The purpose of this guidance is not to tell us how to fast, but to curb excessive enthusiasm, dispel illusions, and help discern subtle temptations from the real problems that may arise. After fasting has become a regular habit, and our guidelines are established through knowledge of ourselves and our weaknesses, the need for supervision diminishes, although it is always wise to have some one person to consult.

Otherwise fasting and prayer, prayer and fasting, are offered in secret. It is one approach to the holy of holies, to claim our inheritance with and in the Christ who dwells in our hearts and cries, "Abba, Father," with the burning love that is his gift to us.

"Out of his infinite glory, may he give you the power through his Spirit for your hidden self to grow strong, so that Christ may live in your hearts through faith, and then, planted in love and built in love, you will with all the saints have strength to grasp the breadth and the length, the height and the depth; until, knowing the love of Christ, which is beyond all knowledge, you are filled with the utter fullness of God."

MARCH

◆

The Face of Love

The Face of Love

Almighty God, we pray you graciously to behold this your family, for whom our Lord Jesus Christ was willing to be betrayed, and given into the hands of sinners, and to suffer death upon the cross; who now lives and reigns with you and the Holy Spirit, one God, for ever and ever. Amen.
—Collect for Good Friday
1979 Book of Common Prayer

Crucifixes are dangerous.

Like many other symbols, they can lose their meaning for us through indifference bred by familiarity. A crucifix is confrontive, and yet we can and often do weasel out of being brought face to face with its message, sometimes in a fit of justifiable rebellion against the lingering Jansenistic piety that, in its imaginative excess, would lay a case of the neurotic guilties on us; or, perhaps while in a failing effort to revivify the significance of the crucifix, we hear a protesting little voice whisper, "But it happened so very long ago, and far away, and somebody else did it."

At the other end of our experiential scale lies a more insidious misuse of the crucifix: in times of distress, in times of crisis when we are feeling put upon and martyred, we sometimes inwardly roll our eyes toward it and heave deep sighs over our hurt, using the sign of selfless immolation to support our selfish wallowing in self-pity.

Crucifixes are dangerous.

Every Lent for the last few years I have sought a remedy for these ills. My Lenten crucifix is not a cross with a corpus on it, but a contemporary photograph, an icon, if you will. No matter what my mood, it does not allow for indifference, or neurotic pseudo guilt. It does not permit me to say, "It happened long ago and far away, and somebody else did it." And most of all, it allows for a deepening entrance into the Passion of Jesus, while obviating any possible vestige of self-pity: its pain is so great, and the shock of it on first viewing so terrible, that you are taken completely out of yourself, and only in steadying against the initial reaction to turn away and look no more does the tremendous and unfathomable mystery of the love of God contained in it become apparent.

Like all true icons, it is the source of ever-deepening contemplation.

The year 1971, when this photograph was taken, is not so long ago, and Japan, where it was taken, is not so far away—no place is very far away in this age of telecommunications, jet transport, and missile-borne nuclear overkill.

And, as principal importers of Japanese products, there is no escaping our involvement in the horror of the events summarized in this picture.

Minamata is a little seacoast town, depending on local waters for its staple food, which is fish. Its major industry, besides fishing, is a large chemical plant supplying basic compounds to Japan's manufacturing complex.

During the late 1960's the people of Minamata began to realize that something was very wrong. The government sent scientists and physicians to investigate the phenomenon known as "Minamata disease." The diagnosis was quite simple, though many were already beyond any cure. The fish on which the people of Minamata subsisted were contaminated with mercury, mercury that the nearby chemical plant had flushed into the estuary, where life in the ocean begins, and as with all such substances, as it became absorbed higher and higher into the food chain, it became increasingly concentrated.

Mercury poisoning is a particularly silent and hideous way of death. Usually by the time it is discovered, the damage is irreversible. It causes retardation, madness, and blindness; the bodies of small children become grotesquely deformed, with twisted limbs and useless nervous systems.

And for many people in Minamata, when the source of their disease was traced to the nearby chemical plant, it was too late.

Eugene Smith traveled to Minamata in 1971 and photographed a Japanese mother bathing her helpless, misshapen child. The picture is so powerful that often one's initial reaction to the distorted figure of the little girl is revulsion, revulsion so intense as to cause physical as well as spiritual nausea.

"Pietà," you tend to register immediately with your brain, and your eyes wish quickly to slip off the edge of the page to something more neutral.

But wait.

Look deeply into this icon.

It is Madonna and Child and Pietà all rolled into one: infinite love, infinite cherishing, infinite sorrow, infinite pain. It is the way God cradles our twisted selves, knowing the evil in them, bathing them with the waters of baptism, and healing them, knowing the agony of distortion we have done to his creation, and yet with tender patience caring for the maimed image of himself, helping us, moving us, washing us into transfiguration. This is an icon of God our Mother, who sees the wholeness in our disfigurement, beauty in our deformity, holiness in our wretchedness.

This blind, contorted girl-child is the Body and figure of Christ, and what we have done to her, we have done to ourselves, and we have done quite literally to him. In her brokenness, in our brokenness, is his brokenness on two pieces of wood, now, not long ago; here, not far away. And we did it. Maybe with a radio. Maybe with a television. Maybe with a piece of clothing.

Made in Japan.

But in the end it adds up to the same pathology as led to Golgotha: envy, power, possessiveness, greed, irreverence, callousness, an appalling preoccupation with the material on a short-term basis.

We tend to think of sin as specific acts we do to others, or propensities we acknowledge in ourselves. We often experience it as general unease and free-floating guilt. But as we begin to understand what the Body of Christ is all about, as we begin to experience in prayer that we are united by and through and with and in him to all creation, and that this creation is of spiritual and material matter that is interchangeable, that is highly mutable, that is charged with the living God, we begin to experience a two-edged sword.

Yes, a kind of ongoing quiet ecstasy of the ordinary, a continuous experience of resurrection, but that is not my focus in Holy Week.

Rather, that my sin and your sin consists not merely in small or big acts within my life, my heart, but that we, you and I, share in every man's sin, and in more than some vague theological way.

I am the pimp on the Minnesota Strip, dealing in young bodies.

I am the pusher, selling drugs to an addict nodding and drooling in the Port Authority Bus Terminal.

I am the mother, scalding and beating and starving my child.

I am the employee ripping off my corporation.

I am the industrialist pouring poison into the bodies, and, by advertising, into the souls, of my brothers.

I am the driver of the nuclear juggernaut, careening wildly out of control toward the last holocaust.

Often I struggle impotently to express this.

Often I would confess these sins as I kneel and gabble my "Bless-me-Father-for-I-have-sinned. . . ." But it is suffering too deep for speech, and true guilt almost too deep for conscious knowledge.

Yet, for all of this, the photograph is also an icon of our life in the blessed Trinity. We are this child, in Christ, looking in unseeing, uncomprehending trust toward God our Mother, and her look of patient love, the long, loving look between us, is the Holy Spirit.

And it is not so much in the tortured body of the child, but in her tender, grieving face, that we see the terrible, aweful price of our redemption.

March

O God, we beg you in your mercy to behold this your family; show us your Face, on which is written the price of your love for us, that by the broken body of your beloved Son we may be healed. Amen.

APRIL

◆

The Resurrecting Word

The Resurrecting Word

A Franciscan friar I know is fond of saying that after the Eucharist we should genuflect to each other because we are all walking tabernacles.

This saying is truer than true, and not only in the half-hour or so following the Liturgy. For by our baptism we are bearers of the living Word, having passed, with Christ, through death to life.

But how do we express this?

We all get very tired of words.

This same friar is fond of reminding me that my tongue is a two-edged sword; my usual retort is that it is not for nothing that I have chosen a life of silence—or rather that it has chosen me. Another of God's little jokes, perhaps. And perhaps the gift of these words is reparation for the other edge.

The Franciscan who confronts me with my Achilles tongue is in good company. Toward the end of my novitiate in a religious community, on my twenty-fourth birthday, the other novices made a card for me, on which was written a quotation from Proverbs: "Death and Life are in the power of the tongue," and on its reverse side they had composed a little Birthday Office, of which the versicle went, "Lord, let her be and keep silent," and the responsory, a heartfelt, "amen, Amen, AMEN!" Little did they know the prophetic nature of their prayer!

In Holy Week, we're brought to an awareness of our share in each other's sin, the sin that caused the tragedy at Minamata, the share we have in the lives of pimp and pusher, child abuser and ripoff artist, corporate extortioner and nuclear huckster.

In Eastertide, we explore the other side of this coin, the other edge of this two-edged sword, as it were, for these edges are hurt and healing, despair and joy, death and life, crucifixion and resurrection. And as we share in each other's sin and guilt too deep to fathom, so, even more, do we share in the resurrection of Christ, and therefore in each other's resurrection.

Charles Williams describes this life in the mystical Body of Christ as coinherence, our being inextricably bound to and in one another, the sharing of and in each other's being in ways that can either destroy or restore. We are not only purveyors of sin, we are also bearers of the resurrecting Word.

That both aspects exist coinherently within our coinhering lives is a great mystery; and that we can choose to tip the balance in either direction, that we can choose which edge of sword we will use, is the perilous gift Christ gives us in our freedom as the children of God.

Scripture is full of references to this sword, and in the Old Testament they are usually references to judgment: the angel with the flaming sword guarding the Garden of Eden; the angel with the sword confronting Balaam's ass; the angel with the sword about to destroy Jerusalem because of David's arrogance at not being content with his lordship over Israel shared out to him by the Lord God, but wanting the lordliness he could derive from his ego by knowing over just how many people he ruled.

In the New Testament the emphasis changes: the angels by the empty tomb have left their swords in heaven; the One who sits on the throne with a sharp two-edged sword coming out of his mouth says, "Do not be afraid. I am the first and the last, and I am the living one; for I was dead and now I am alive for evermore, and I hold the keys of Death and Death's domain."

Fear not, for judgment is given from the throne of the crucified One.

For he is the Word come to us ". . . living and active, sharper than any two-edged sword, piercing to the division of soul and spirit, of joints and marrow, and discerning the thoughts and intentions of the heart." Like the shaft of light in an eye surgeon's laser that can repair a detached retina, and is sharper than any scalpel, the divine Word, crucified and risen, can penetrate to the deepest places of our selves to fuse our fragmentation, to glorify our wounds, to bring us from the death we share into the resurrection we share; to graft in us himself, that we may bear him to bring his fruitful peace, to be to each other the resurrected Christ, bearers of the resurrecting Word.

And as in vineyard grafting, we, the rootstock, must be cut to the heart by Christ the Word, in order that his fruitful bud may be attached, and our mingled lives grow in coinherence. For "No branch can bear fruit by itself, but only if it remains united with the vine; no more can you bear fruit, unless you remain united with me."

It was only one spring, years after that long-ago convent birthday, that I discovered that my sisters had given me only half the quotation from Proverbs. The whole reads, "Death and Life are in the power of the tongue, and those who love it will eat its fruits." Or, in the NEB translation, "The tongue has power of life and death; make friends with it and enjoy its fruits."

We must be wounded deeply to bear these fruits, to have Christ grafted in us, to be grafted in him. And let's not kid ourselves. We all are the walking wounded. We walk around with all our hurts showing, and though we may think we hide our brokenness, it is especially in our life together that we see each other's vulnerability, see each other's *vulnera*, or wounds, and have the choice of which edge of the sword we will use: the edge of destruction and death, or the edge of healing and life.

Or, even more awesome, we have the invitation to be open enough to Christ and to one another to allow the resurrecting Word, the shaft of Light and Life that is sharper than any sword, to pour through us, to become incarnated within us, to allow God to pray us for each other to fuse our fragmented selves. And the way to this openness is by acknowledging our wounds, by loving our wounds, so that they coinhere with our Lord's glorious wounds, and through them, through our own wounds now sharing in his glory, our brother or sister—and our selves—can be healed.

If we can bring ourselves to take this risk, to allow this healing to take place through our own bleeding hurts, through our sharing in one another's passion, it means that we really begin to understand what the glory of the Cross is all about: that it makes us guilt-free, not in a pseudo-psychoanalytic sense of never feeling guilty about anything at all, but in the resurrected sense of knowing the truth of our guilt, and the joy of its being taken completely away.

And just as this resurrected Word has been given to each of us, so we can give it to each other. When we forgive each other, it means that we forgive wholly. So often when we go about forgiving we want to make sure that the other person is left with just enough residual guilt that he or she really knows how much our precious egos have been hurt. But that is not what the healing radiance of the crucifixion is all about.

It is about enabling each other to be guilt-free as Christ's death has enabled us to be guilt-free. In our daily life it means taking the risk of the fool: to offer love at the risk of having it rejected; to offer to share pain at the risk of having our own wounds reopened; to forgive so that the other person is guilt-free at the risk of having to forgive all over again; of placing ourselves, our lives, in the other person's hands in radical trust.

And beyond reason. If there is one hard lesson that Holy Week and Easter teaches us, it is that we have to learn to love, hope, forgive, and trust beyond any rational base, not in the wildly extravagant gesture made by Margaret Fuller who reportedly said to Emerson, "I *accept* the universe!" to which Carlyle, to whom this remark was conveyed, replied, "Gad, she'd better!" but in the most ordinary speech and action of our lives together. That at each moment we can choose death for each other or life for each other; that at each moment we can risk new pain but also new life by offering our very selves for and to each other.

To be able to do this involves radical listening, a constant attentiveness to the still, small voice of God who constantly speaks within us, and through the people around us if only we will hear. In the introduction of her translation of *The Sayings of the Desert Fathers*, Benedicta Ward describes the process by which a hermit went to his abba, or to an elder, for direction. "The Sayings," she writes, "were more than words of advice or instruction; they were words given by a spiritual father to his sons as life-giving words that would bring them to salvation."

And in her definition of the Greek word *apothegm*, or saying, she writes, " 'Give me a word' is a key phrase in the desert tradition. The 'word' is not an explanation or a consoling suggestion; it is a word that is truly life-giving if it is not discussed or argued over, but simply received and integrated into life."

And the silent, unspoken question that continually underlies *our* life together as we pass each other in a corridor, or talk casually in the course of daily life is, "Brother, Sister, do you have a word for me? Give me a word. Give me a word of healing; give me a word of life; give me a word of resurrection."

How often, in response, do we speak a resurrecting word? How often a word of condemnation?

Many of us have poor self-images, and therefore poor images of each other. So, to turn the question around, how often do we greet one another as the image and likeness of God, with the reverence and joy that calls forth the Word, that enables the other to be vulnerable and unafraid, and speak the word of life?

For we are all called to be abbas and ammas for each other, and more: we are called to be Christs for each other. This is the glory and dread of our vocations as Christians: that he may become incarnated within each of us, that we may bear the resurrecting Word, the Word of Life.

And this Word is a celebration. A priest friend of mine puts it this way: "The Passion and Crucifixion are the glorification of the Son in whom the glory of God is revealed. We must not think the Resurrection is that glorification. The Resurrection is the great celebration *after* the glory has been revealed. It is a frightening glory."

The most powerful experience I have had of this celebration was during a retreat in which I was involved at a Roman Catholic monastery. Never in my life, in the colloquia, in individual conferences, have I shared so much laughter, so many tears of pain and joy, in so short a week. On one of the last days, at one of the colloquia, there was a break when we were given a little awareness exercise to do with a cup of tea, individually, and off by ourselves.

I went outside to a nearby hermitage, and, after the exercise, stood there drinking my tea, looking across the valley at the line of mountains. I was feeling increasingly helpless, and turning over and over in my mind was the question, "How can I possibly receive all of this overwhelming love?"

The next morning, the subject in the colloquium was the lawyer who tried to trap Jesus, and the parable of the Good Samaritan. The question we explored was the love of God, neighbor, self, and my own struggle was to know this love as one seamless love, not three loves, or one love taking a couple of acute-angle turns, as we often experience it.

But a few hours later at the Eucharist I received the answer to both my questions. The new Roman rite retains the prayer, "Lord, I am not worthy to receive you; speak but the word and I shall be healed."

Suddenly I understood that each monk in the colloquia, each monk I passed in the hall, each monk with whom I shared those moments of joy and tears, was not only, to use the Franciscan friar's phrase, a walking tabernacle, not only bore the glorified and resurrected Christ, but at the heart of this mystery truly *was* Christ, and that in our sharing of our wounds, our laughter and sorrow, our silliness and wisdom, the Word was indeed spoken and we were healed.

And from then on, as we encountered one another, these words echoed in my heart: "Edward (or William, or Gerald, or Andrew . . .), I am not worthy to receive you."

Reader, I am not worthy to receive you; speak but the Word, the resurrecting Word, the Word of life, the Word of love you bear, and we both shall be healed.

Saint Mark's Penance

Most of us, at some point, experience the sharply poignant tension between our own needs and compassion, between the instinct toward self-preservation and our desire to lay down our life for our friend. As we grow into God, our needs become compassion, or, to put it another way, the exercise of compassion fulfills all of our needs.

While modern psychology has given us many useful tools for discovering the self we must deny, the ego we must give up, to be Jesus' disciple, it has also, in its popularized form, led to a certain amount of unhealthy involution, self-justification, and the theology of excuse.

There are few more effective cures for navel-gazing than a confrontive confessor.

Some years ago, before creeping cultural narcissism became a national epidemic, I was making an uncomfortable readjustment to the use of the Sacrament of Reconciliation, and my confessor, being a wise and creative man, suggested I needed something more than the usual psalm or prayer for a penance. "Meditate," he said that memorable St. Mark's day, "on paper on the relationship between analysis and reparation."

Although the sentences that follow set analysis (whether psychoanalysis or other forms of analysis) and reparation in ironic opposition to each other, they are, in fact, complementary.

This is not a paradox. Both have a vocational quality to them (especially if you are talking about people coming to terms with their own personal solitude). There is a sense in which certain basic distinctions have to be made in and about life before reparation can become viable in a practical way in the Christian life.

This does not mean that full self-disclosure must occur before reparation is possible: the invitation to reparation unfolds as the real self becomes apparent, and the mechanisms of the superficial self are exposed.

It is necessary to begin to understand what the human condition is and does before you can understand how it is intensified in each member of the Body of Christ.

So that reparation builds on analysis, but goes far beyond it in a synergesis with faith, offering the whole complex of human pain and suffering and sin in transcendent simplicity.

Analysis is a tearing apart so reconstruction can take place.
Reparation is taking everything, torn apart, reconstructed, unreconstructed, to heart.

Analysis judges and sorts out.
Reparation accepts.

Analysis justifies.
Reparation stands accused.

Analysis teaches you to distinguish healthy guilt from neurotic guilt and often leaves you guilt-free.
Reparation accepts all guilt for everything and everyone.

Analysis teaches you to deal with pain and your own problems, to live relatively pain-free and avoid or handle pain-causing situations.
Reparation takes on others' pain, not only receiving it as given, but also praying to be allowed to share pain, to bear it for and instead of.

Analysis disperses pain by talking about it.
Reparation receives pain by listening, bearing it in silence, and offering it in love to the Father.

Analysis teaches you how to choose people who will be beneficial to you.

Reparation teaches you to kiss lepers.

Analysis teaches you the ruthless pursuit of goodness.

Reparation teaches you above all to love, to open yourself so that Love can pour through you, and that nothing else matters.

Analysis tells you that by shaping yourself up, you will shape up everyone you know.

Reparation shows you that by healing yourself, by finding your wholeness in God, healing is poured out on creation.

Analysis teaches you to solve problems by reasoning, verbalizing, and manipulating, through focusing on your feelings.

Reparation teaches you to bear and offer problems in prayer and fasting beyond words, action, or reason, in thanksgiving.

Analysis gives you armor against your enemies.

Reparation makes you utterly vulnerable.

Analysis discovers the mechanisms of the false self.

Reparation releases the mechanisms of the real self in Christ.

Analysis teaches you that you are Somebody Special.

Reparation teaches you that you are nobody and nothing.

Analysis gives you the tools for living in the world.

Reparation takes the consequences.

Analysis teaches you to display yourself.

Reparation teaches you to hide yourself.

Analysis helps you to explain.

Reparation offers none.

Analysis teaches you to trust your instincts.
Reparation teaches you to trust everyone.

Analysis makes you self-sufficient.
Reparation makes you dependent on God alone.

Analysis teaches you to be successful.
Reparation teaches you to be destitute.

Analysis releases creativity.
Reparation releases forgiveness.

Analysis helps you to find yourself.
Reparation helps you to lose yourself.

Analysis gives you permission.
Reparation sets you free.

Analysis teaches you your limits.
Reparation teaches you there are no limits.

Analysis teaches self-assertion.
Reparation teaches self-denial.

Analysis teaches you to grasp.
Reparation teaches you to let go.

Analysis defines.
Reparation adores.

Analysis teaches you to live so you can die.
Reparation teaches you to die so you can live.

MAY

◆

Chastity

Chastity

Almighty God, to you all hearts are open, all desires known, and from you no secrets are hid; cleanse the thoughts of our hearts by the inspiration of your Holy Spirit, that we may perfectly love you and worthily magnify your holy Name; through Jesus Christ our Lord. Amen.

—Eucharistic Collect
1979 Book of Common Prayer

When I made my solemn vows, the third of the four questions the bishop asked began as follows: "Are you willing to remain celibate and unmarried for the sake of the kingdom of God, and, after the example of Christ, to grow in chastity, that is, purity of heart?" The wording of this question has been the source of a lot of ribald humor, and rightly so. It's symbolic of the latter part of the twentieth century to have to be asked if you are willing to remain celibate as well as unmarried for the sake of the Kingdom of Heaven!

Chastity, though, whether married chastity or celibate chastity, is no joke, and both marriage and celibacy are empty unless they are tied to chastity. Thus, when I use this word, I mean the thrust toward a single-minded love and search for God in both expressions of life.

So much negative claptrap has been written about chastity that it is almost impossible to debunk it all. And such refutation would be futile.

Simply put, chastity is an act of adoration.

In its most primitive interpretation, chastity has meant for the married person to remain monogamous, and for the celibate to refrain from sexual activity in relationships. On this crude level it's the *one* vow we can know for sure whether we've kept or broken.

If these rather tiresome strictures were all there is to chastity, then it, too, would be empty and joyless. But chastity is more, much more. It's the agent of joy and the balm for healing our divided hearts. It's the means by which we learn to embrace all of life, wholeheartedly, in exaltation and suffering, and to go out to meet our Lord and our life in his divine embrace as he has taught us, with arms outstretched.

Chastity enables God to preoccupy us increasingly with himself, so that we begin to learn that we pray with our whole life; so that we become increasingly, consciously and unconsciously, in union with the prayer of Christ, which is the only prayer there is.

We delude ourselves that we pray: he only prays. Our act we call prayer is yielding to him and his prayer springing from the molten core of his love within us. As this prayer becomes more and more deeply rooted in our lives, we begin to learn wholeheartedness.

Brother David Steindl-Rast has spoken about this prayer of wholeheartedness. He says that anything we do with a whole heart is prayer. By way of example, he recommends that if, when you come home from a long day, you are too tired to say an Office, to pray a shower. I've taken great comfort in this advice, and have prayed many showers, gardens, walks, and conversations with cats and other beasts with my slowly healing heart.

Wholeheartedness includes the Buddhist concept of mindfulness, but goes much farther. It means not only that when you wash the dishes you wash the dishes, but also that when you talk with someone your heart and mind are united with theirs as you focus on communication, communion, of one being with another; it means that when you make love you make love with your whole being, spontaneously giving and receiving, with tenderness and laughter and passion, not with your mind divorced by sanctimonious piety from your body which is going through the motions!

Purity is not prudery.

We have to stop asking the questions "Is this prayer?" and "Am I praying?" with all the dualistic and legalistic assumptions implicit in them and ask, instead, "How is this moment of my life, this action, *not* prayer?" Or better yet, not think to ask at all. We have to open all our life to the mystery of Christ's prayer that *is* our life, and, when we see obvious ways in which our life isn't prayer in a particular moment, to move immediately to compunction.

We have so distorted what chastity is all about that creeping Manicheanism has dominated the Church's teaching for centuries. It's no wonder we've had a sexual revolution. But now a curious thing is happening: as with all revolutions, the momentum is beginning to reverse itself, and there is evidence of a new movement toward celibacy in secular life, especially among single people.

No doubt this secular celibacy has the potential to lead us into a renewal of the errors of which we have just rid ourselves, and prissiness may once again rear its simpering head. It's almost worse than sexual license.

If I were deciding on a marriage partner, or deciding who would be admitted to a monastery, you can be sure that I would rather have a tired tart than a smug virgin.

This is not to say that there are not rare people who learn to give wholly while remaining technical virgins all their lives: there are many illustrations in the lives of the officially canonized saints and others, like Newton, to show that this can occur. But, like the saints, they are few and far between.

For the rest of us who, for better or worse, take a different way into the mercy of God, there is a kind of giving and a kind of pain, a kind of fulfillment and a kind of loneliness that brings us face to face with our own solitude and hunger for God learned only through sexual relationships of whatever kind.

This is *not* to say that a young person should be told to wait to marry or become a monk until he or she has gone out specifically to lose his or her virginity. The alarming statistics of teenage pregnancy and suicide evidence that young people, often pressured by a promiscuous culture, are damaged and left without wonder or delight or hope at an increasingly early age.

But it seems to be a fact of life that most of us are cases of arrested development without sexual experience of some kind, without the experience of deep commitment and deep betrayal, and deeper forgiveness and capacity for compassion that ideally grow from these haunted relationships of sin and redemption at the heart of our mortality.

For we all make commitments; we all betray them in one way or another; and to live with ourselves, we must learn to forgive and to be forgiven, to be reconciled with the other person and with our own actions.

It is in the process of suffering through these relationships that we learn what commitment is all about, that we begin to learn the price of loving, hoping, forgiving, and trusting beyond any rational base, even if the relationship, to an individual or a community, comes to an end.

It is this gut knowledge that grows and strengthens marriage vows and religious vows, and these vows are worth precious little without the purification of this learning to adore through the incomprehensible events of life, through the crucifixion of despair that we all inevitably experience.

A wise man once told me that we all get crucified in the end, and that one might as well be crucified for one's own ideals as for someone else's.

In saying this, I'm not advocating going against the teaching of the Church; I'm merely pointing out the facts of our psychological and spiritual life, that, as Bishop Paul Moore has said, just as we invariably rebel against our earthly family as part of the process of psychological maturation, so, with a few rare exceptions, we also rebel against our heavenly family and our heavenly Father as part of the process of spiritual maturation.

It is an intrinsic part of growing up, of finding our identity, of establishing our self and taking responsibility for it; of finding out who we really are, so that when it comes time to give, we have a self *to* give, so that when we enter a relationship our love is not possessive, trying to put on someone else's self, but coinhering, that is not an obliteration of self in the other person's tastes and opinions in unhealthy dependency, but rather, as the poet Rilke says, a meeting of two solitudes who can afford ". . . the extravagance of walking unembraced."

The end point of learning to live from neither submission nor rebellion, which comes with self-knowledge, is the beginning of freedom, of relinquishing our defenses, of giving up sweet anger and blame and self-righteousness, of letting go the pleasure of seeing the mote in the other's eye, while ignoring the six by twelve in our own.

It is the beginning of living passionately, of living *compassionately*, in the literal sense of that word: the letting go of judgment to be crucified with the other. The agony of the other lives in your own heart because you wholeheartedly, in self-forgetfulness, share your being with the other in living intercession.

Here is where we come to the essence of what marriage and religious vows, which are extensions of our baptismal vows, are all about: to enable us to come to that meeting place where in dread and awe and love we meet our God alone, and do not run screaming in terror in the other direction.

Poverty, whether experienced through simplicity or surfeit, makes us know our need of God, enables us to begin stripping from our lives all that interferes with our being drawn to him in his wooing of us. Obedience, the giving, constant giving in love, of our selves for others, means that we grow in yielding to his gentle summons in our hearts. And chastity, chastity above all in its fidelity, leads us into the adoration which is all of our life lived in self-forgetfulness—and who has not tasted self-forgetfulness, this greatest gift of love, of fulfillment, without hungering after it with increasing desire?

Chastity leads us to the purity of heart that in Kierkegaard's words is "to will one thing," the increasing focus of living for God alone and not self.

Chastity is the physical response of our inadequate love to the overwhelming and unbearable love and mercy of a God who loves us not only in our weakness but also at our worst, a love that is so painful in its enfolding of us (painful because it is pure and we are not) that the only possible response is with our whole incarnate being.

Chastity is the orgasm of prayer.*

This is as true for the lay person as the monk, for the married person as the single person.

There is no use for any vows if the motivation is not the love and adoration of this God who is love, and a total focusing of our lives in him. As one grows in prayer, the need for chastity becomes increasingly evident: our God is indeed a consuming fire, and to live under this vow in monastic life, for example, implicitly in the novitiate or actually as professed, and at the same time engage in physical promiscuity or promiscuity of the heart, causes deeply rooted conflicts which, if not dealt with, eventuate in the person's leaving community and/or other serious psychological, physical, and spiritual problems. You cannot make this vow with your fingers crossed, or with sub-clauses and exceptions.

Promiscuity also causes conflicts within the community, and the tragedy is that those affected may not be the ones engaged in the behavior, but rather those who feel most guilty in themselves about the betrayal of the vow.

In our practical working out of chastity we have made some ludicrous mistakes. We have at times attempted outwardly to deny that God created us male and female, and buried married and religious women and men in a kind of asexual purdah, substituting elaborate social restrictions and monastic veneer to protect ourselves from the very real risks of going out to meet life—the precious gift God has given us to delight in—with open arms and an open heart.

Neither married nor religious life is an escape. Marriage is not for those who fear homosexuality or solitude, because sooner or later one must come to terms with the masculine or feminine side of oneself, and one's own personal solitude, from which one learns to love and give.

Nor is religious life a refuge for those who fear the opposite sex, or being with other people, for here, too, a woman becomes a harpy if she does not embrace and integrate her masculine

---

*A Trappist abbot points out the reversibility of this koan: prayer is the orgasm of chastity.

side, and a man is emasculated if he does not embrace and integrate his feminine side. And as every hermit knows, you are never less alone than when you are in solitude.

The commandment we have been given is to love God, neighbor, and self—*all* of one's self—with the same love, because it is the same breath of God that flames life into our neighbor and our selves as feeds the fires of the blessed Trinity.

And God has a sense of humor. A Franciscan who was a real spiritual father to me used to say that God loves a good dirty joke—not a crude dirty joke, but one that has some elegance and irony to it. I've always thought it one of God's better jokes that he created our plumbing equipment in such close concert with our reproductive organs.

But we mustn't fool ourselves. Chastity is difficult. And as we become more attuned to the love of God, as we become more mindful of the beauty of his creation, and as our sense becomes more acute because we are enabled to see that each leaf, each creature, each human being is limned with fire, so the fires of our hearts are stirred, and we respond with our bodies as part of our whole being.

Sublimation in its best sense can occur and does, but, even if we've learned repeatedly through bitter experience that surfeit—whether of food or sex or power—is useless to satisfy that hollow feeling within us, the hunger that grows with true knowledge of God, there is always the temptation to try to substitute these things, to sedate our hearts and our hunger, even though we know very well that short-term gratification is fleeting and ultimately fails, leaving us more desolate and unsatisfied than before, for we are increasingly restless until we rest in him.

And while physical chastity, like fasting, is best learned and practiced without making an issue out of it, there are, nevertheless, nights and days when we simply have to sweat it out, laughing at ourselves, giving thanks that everything is still in good working order. And as we grow older, this sudden being seized by desire and delight can be a reaffirmation of the intensity with which we are giving back to God the life he has given us, and a blessing.

In doing this it is crucial to understand that there is a big difference between saying, "No, I won't do that," and trying to repress or deny or psychically cut off (as Origen did physically) what God in his goodness has given us. One is asceticism born of love; the other is heresy. And where sexuality has been killed, spirituality withers and dies.

There is no gainsaying that in this stance we are in complete opposition to secular culture and certain trends in contemporary monastic culture. There is an attitude abroad that says anything that causes discomfort is bad and should be rid from life. Somehow we have come to apply a double standard to the monastic life, both within and without, which makes monastic chastity somehow "harder" or more "sick" than married chastity, or no chastity at all, so much so that there is a prevailing notion that it's more neurotic and destructive for a horny monk or sister to endure the suffering involved in remaining focused on God through celibate chastity than it is for a horny husband or wife to endure the suffering involved in remaining focused on God through married chastity.

It's ironic that in a culture where high value is placed on the kind of suffering involved in personal narcissisms (e.g., sports) the suffering involved in personal growth in self-discipline is suspect. We religious tend to complain at the least pain or discomfort, harboring, perhaps, a martyred view of ourselves. This is hardly following Christ—who ever said a cross wasn't going to be lonely, depressing, difficult, and painful?

(I can see my Franciscan father now, shaking his head slightly as he says with his cadaverous twinkle, "It's always the wrong cross, Brother, always the wrong cross.")

At the same time we can see in this attitude the struggle to find a corrective to the negative—almost Gnostic—approach to asceticism that has prevailed for centuries, a struggle to understand that true asceticism can grow only from a theology of affirmation, of love of God's goodness, truth, and beauty that is so deep, and which wordless understanding has pushed us so far that it *must*, it *demands* asceticism because any distractions from this apophatic vision of God renders this stage of life, this unblinking gaze, torment. It is in this purifying fire of affirmation of the goodness of *all* that God has made that we rest in him, not in the denial of what is most precious at the heart of our mortality.

Perhaps one of the lessons among the many to be learned here is that the struggle to remain chaste is not the same as the conflict caused by promiscuity within the vowed life. The first is the normal tension of any religious or married life, of striving and constantly falling short; the second is a basic violation of personal integrity.

The lack of wise and compassionate education in chastity, of spiritual counsel, and community support of one another in this area leads to the breaking down of fidelity in times of crises—fidelity to the relationships that bind the community together.

Certainly vows in religious community imply "for better or worse" as much as married vows (and would that people had a marriage novitiate), not the attitude we've seen so much of lately of "As soon as the going gets rough I'm bailing out" or "I'll stick around until and unless something better comes along."

The ramifications of chastity are deeply tied to personal integrity, fidelity to self, fidelity to community, and, above all, fidelity to the search for God. If casually regarded, it becomes one of the basic sources of conflict within each person and within community life. This is as true outside monastic life as within it, because each of us is one day brought to the point, if we are in any way searching for God, when we can no longer do what we want, but what we must, giving up the lesser goods for the greatest good, the pearl of great price.

Cold comfort, maybe, that it doesn't get any easier as we grow older. But God weans us from the seduction of the material, and as beautiful as created things increasingly become, they are not worth the price we pay for the possession of them, which is the interruption, the frustration of our adoration, of our self-forgetfulness, of our acquiring the experiential knowledge that love is the union of wills and not feelings only, the union of our true selves.

It is our true individuation, with the deepening, dark, obscure, yet ever more alive perception of him, a dynamic relationship that is oblique, yet more vibrant and alive than any transient sense of his immediate presence. A relationship that demands all of us, our faithfulness to risk, our freedom from everything, even, in the end, from the sacrament of earthly life.

Chastity, however, and fidelity to it also brings a certain fecundity, a certain kind of parenting that is as true of celibate chastity as it is of married chastity.

There is in chastity and its motivation, its signification of single-hearted love, a kind of knowledge—a *gnosis* if you will, but a true *gnosis*—of the freedom that comes with this purifying fire that transforms eros, crucified, yes, but resurrected too, and resurrected in the fullest sense of the new creation which reproduces itself *now.*

Those who are faithful are guardians of this fire, and it is only by their fidelity that they parent, pass on this flame. It is a very real kind of apostolic succession, the passing on of goodness, the passing on of the resurrection, the reproduction of the resurrection in the next generation each member of which, in turn, must be converted, convinced, parented, not by words only but by the example of chastity lived out. Each must be set ablaze with love. And there is only us to send.

Chastity lies at the central paradox of Christianity, of death into life, of deserts bursting into bloom; of the transfiguration of creation; of balanced wholeness. Lying as it does at the center of the incarnate person, of our bodies, it is intrinsic to sense of self and therefore sense of communion, and with communion in the deepest sense comes the mandate to disseminate, to bear fruit. The fruit of chastity is fertile, gives fertility by the very ashes of its fire. It is bound to creativity, to focused life-energy, to new creation, to bringing new creation and the Kingdom into being. This fire is the salt and savor of all creation, this apophatic fire, Hidden-Word-Spirit, Trinitarian core that is at once most unknowable and continually breaking out through creation.

Something happened at Mass one day that summed up a little of this interplay of forces at work in the living-out of chastity. I was watching a priest celebrate the Eucharist at fairly close quarters. He celebrated with such an unconscious beauty, with such deftness and sureness, tenderness and strength that the thought—not a fantasy or temptation or anything of that nature—just the words crossed my mind, as naturally and ordinarily as any other reflection: "I wonder if he makes love like that?"

Blasphemy? No. What is the Eucharist if not love-making in its largest sense; and, dare we to say it, what is love-making, in its greatest sense, if not Eucharist? I wish someone, not a lifelong celibate, would write a book called *Lovemaking and the Eucharist.*

At the time of my profession, a Trappist hermit wrote, "I've been reading a bit about Catherine of Genoa recently.... On one occasion after receiving Communion she was aware of so much sweetness that it was almost like heaven. She turned to our Lord and told Him plainly, 'Do you intend to draw me with these things? I don't want them. I want You. And I want all of You.'

"That makes me think of you," he went on, referring to the fact that I was making my profession without knowing where my next hermitage would be, without knowing where I was going. And what he wrote next applies to us all, for, in truth, none of us knows what lies ahead. "On the secondary level," he said, "there are elements of uncertainty. But at the deepest level, at the heart of the matter there is definiteness. For you know Whom you want. And you know in Whom you believed. May He be with you...."

In the end, though, I turn to Rilke, who perhaps understands these complexities better than most:

While life still takes and gives and takes again,
from give and take we keep originating:
creatures so shadowy, changing, fluctuating,
yet in our heart of hearts so very fain

to go through this eternal self-displacing
bravely, erectly, unimpeachably;
from day to night, from night to day set racing—
we through whom life upsprings incessantly

from our own living, blood from our own veins,
joy from our joyance, grief from our own grieving,

all which we all at once are once more leaving
because our lonely soul already deigns

to go before us. . . .

My darkness, my darkness, I'm standing with you,
and all goes outwardly by;
and I would that in me as in beasts there grew
one voice, one single cry for it all. . . .

If I pile my heart on my brain and my own
longing thereon and my being-alone,
how small it's grown,
since *He* so far transcends.

. . . . for what can these words avail
that come but will not abide,
when the call of a bird in the juniper vale,
cried, and again outcried,
has all the world and my heart like this
and the fear of death and Heaven's bliss,
almost to Him, inside . . .

Let it only, though,
find some abiding place and not be so
lost in that space which they can hardly bear,
those stars of yours: for it is falling there. . . .
You let your own saints' hearts slip quietly away
into the very wretchedest enfolding:
they bloomed there and bore fruit without delay.

You great incomprehensible expender,
as in a single bound you pass me by.
You gleaming stag!
                    . . . . go ever lightlier fleeing
through your pursuers . . .
but they, Unreachable, are only seeing
the parted world behind you reunite.

Rainer Maria Rilke

JUNE

◆

Big Sur Diptych I
Summer Solstice

So we do not lose heart. Though our outer nature is wasting away, our inner nature is being renewed every day. For this slight momentary affliction is preparing for us an eternal weight of glory beyond all comparison, because we look not to the things that are seen but to the things that are unseen; for the things that are seen are transient, but the things that are unseen are eternal.

—*2 Corinthians 4:16–18*

The Hebrew word for "glory," as in "the glory of God," is *kavod*. It carries the nuance of weight, of destiny. This gives an idea of holiness entirely apposite to the Greek notion, which is the way in which we commonly think of it, as if the holier something is the more ethereal it is.

But the Hebrew is more accurate and, like many mystical insights, is also consonant with today's physics, which tells us that space-time is bent by the mass of concentrated energy-become-matter such as our earth, such as a human being.

The Big Sur Diptychs were written when this idea of holiness-as-density had just burst into my small universe of understanding. It has become for me an implicit assumption underlying much of my theology. I had always been suspicious of the Greek melting-into-nothingness anyway: it was too much thought and not enough evidence; too little incarnate reality.

I don't understand physics enough to hope to explore all the ramifications of this idea of *kavod*; perhaps the Red Bull, the Psalm-Singers, Star Fox and the lightnings and fogs of the Vigil will arouse the interest of someone more competent than I to further explore these endless reaches of light.

The Red Bull

Last evening on my way to the hermitage I saw a coyote leap out of the junk pile at the dump. The hair stood up on my neck; I watched him disappear in the pines, and as I approached, I saw him again, leaping through the high, dry grass. There was the sense of other life about, and as I rounded the corner I saw a huge cow, bulging with an unborn calf.

Cows almost wrecked another hermitage of mine before I got an enclosure fence up; these are strays from the next ranch. There must be a fence down along the creek in the canyon.

Fearful for my tent, I pick up pieces of earth and small rocks and start pelting the cow to get her to move off down the mountain, back across the creek. She is strangely unmoved.

Something deep within me gives a warning, and I turn, and not twenty feet away, just below the brow of the hill, is an enormous red bull, shaking his head in disapproval at my treatment of his cow. With him are four other cows, more flighty and nervous than the one I have been assaulting.

In spite of my fear, I am transfixed. This is no ordinary domestic bull, lumpish and dull, or hopelessly nervous and insane. This is the bull I met on a hike last January, but the winter on the mountain has hardened him. He is secure in his power. Who knows what he has encountered in those months? I have seen him climbing vertical slopes; seen him on the way to water at the creek. Has he fought coyotes off from newborn calves, and encountered the cougar after an easy meal?

The red of his hide is intensified by the red-gold of the evening light; there is a sheen to it like kimono silk, like the red-gold of the silk embroidery on an obi I once had. His muscles are hard and flat and smooth under the taut skin; his eyes are clear under his straight horns. He is relaxed and yet alert; coiled potential, and yet unrealized. He is vitality, virility, eros and yet eros transcending itself into beauty. He is the love of God in creation, become eros, and transmuted again into something more than creation, into the hidden fire revealed in creation. I have entered the myth of the bull.

Here is a bull to dance with, straight horns to grasp and vault over in ecstasy, in joy, grasping dread and death, grasping mortality, yet transcending it with mortality. Here is a bull to charge the senses, to communicate the very life-ness of things. . . .

I speak to him, apologizing for my aggression to his cow, and he resumes eating, watching me out of the corner of his eye. I slip down through the pines to the hermitage, make a few adjustments in case there is a cattle raid in revenge, and once again climb up through the dark passage in the pines. He is there: startled this time as I emerge, his head jerks up. I speak to him again, and he relaxes and resumes eating. But every ten feet of my progress past him is marked by his raising his head, making sure I will behave myself in his presence. I have broken protocol, not enough to be charged, but enough to be put on warning. I avert my eyes to lessen any possible interpretation of aggression, and quietly pass him and go down to the monastery for the night. I am not brave enough to risk meeting him in the dark on the way to midnight vigils. Behind me he resumes eating, glowing in the evening light.

All night and next morning I am caught by the bull. I dance with him in my dreams. At dawn I return to my tent, but he is gone and the cows with him: no vengeance taken for my intrusion. The myths of the Greeks and Cretans come consciously to mind now: Zeus and Europa; the frescoes of red bulls at Knossos; Mary Renault's *The King Must Die*, which I have read again and again. Now I understand: now I understand the bull-calf at Horeb, the yearning for that vitality, that sign of potency and life in the desert. Now I understand the making of bull-gods, the seemingly suicidal bull-dances of the Mediterranean, and, by extension, the bloody rituals in Spain. Suits of light pass through my mind, and black Muria bulls charge into the ring.

Pagan: I am pagan, if this is paganism, and thank God for it.

It is a genius of Christianity, perhaps, that primordial religion is the foundation of the sacred. These created signs of Incarnation—arrows pointing to that Event two thousand years ago. And arrows pointing toward it, perhaps, before that Event, just as there is more than a chronological appropriateness of reading certain scriptural passages in the light of the present feast (today's Trinity, and the first letter of John, for example), and the naturalness of it, the Spirit's activity recapitulating in our own lives the events and mysteries of these special days. This is the pagan sense baptized in the Light; the unity of all things, the immanence of God and his utter transcendence.

Though I have repeated it until I am tired of hearing it, there are not four loves, nor two; there is only One. And I have seen this Love in an unspeakable way in the bull: the transmutation of this Love; its forms and expressions; its earthiness and in that very earthiness, the potency of the bull, its mortality transcended. I feel as mute, as clumsy, as tongue tied to describe this as I am other forms of Apophatic Fire. Yet the Word seeks expression, even though in moving from *gnosis* to fumbling concepts most of what we have been given is lost.

Man moves inward: this is his movement. And gazing on and united to that apophatic Face of fire he is expanded by it, bursting out of bondage into boundlessness, unable to be contained, hurled outward by the force, the divine energy, the Fire (God's movement is outward); and even his body cannot contain it: the light of union. It shines in the glory of the human face. It is the glory of God become the glory of the human face.

And as the density of his *point vierge* increases, as the glory builds in intensity, it has no choice but to break out of mortality, just as the fruit tree's fire is the sign of its fruitfulness, its fullness, seeds fallen into the ground, and yet the fire of leaves, which will fall, too, and become dust, somehow expand the spectrum, become the spectrum of color so broad and so intense that it cannot but resolve into white light beyond, across mortality. There is a link, an inseparable bond between our physiochemistry and our divinity. It is not a dualism. And the incarnateness, the very earthiness, earthliness, express the transfiguration within.

Thus it is not a "waste" or cause for cynicism that man

bursts into flame, comes to wisdom and fruition toward the end of his life, only to die. He can do no other: by the fruitfulness of his contemplative being alone he has expanded beyond the containment of mortality: he cannot but die.

The glory within him arcs across the barriers of death, deep calling to Deep, to finally and fully merge with the Glory of the Creator. The Father gives incarnateness with one hand, the fire and the glory with the other. What does it matter what the man has "accomplished" or "done" or what tangible "fruit" he has borne? No matter. And literally so. No matter. Because it is the fullness of the curvature of space-time he has made with his being that counts; the fullness with which he has gathered that density, focused his capacity for that density, by his being, by his acceptance of his being and his fate. By receiving and glorying in his mortality, in the god-ness, the likeness, the image that is caught for a time in his mortality, in the *beauty* of mortality as well as its terror and dreadfulness. The veil is no more.

Thus it is that red-goldness of fruition links all creation: the redness of the bull; the leaves on fire of fruit trees and squalid old poison oak become burning bushes; the joyousness of birdsong at dawn and dusk; the ruddiness in the faces of old men and women; the red-and-gold silk vestments with which we celebrate the blood of the martyrs, who became Bread for us; who were consumed with fire—the fire of St. Ignatius (of Antioch) and the fire of the Love which poured through them; the fire of Trinity: the dynamic of the wheel of Love flaming from Person to Person to Person, and in our center.

O Trinity of blessed light: your fiery sun goes its way, spreading the red-gold of light diffused through our mortality, through the life-giving atmosphere, to remind us that beyond the darkness is another day. O Unity of princely might, the flame-colors of evening speak to us of fruition, of the tiredness of time spent, bodies spent, lives spent in your Day, in your Love. With night our weary bodies sink down, and our restless spirits contemplate your mysteries in our dreams; united to you our sleep is healing of body and spirit. Father, we rest in You; Son, we dance with You; Spirit, we burn with You. Bring us into the fire of your Life. *Amen.*

The Psalm-Singers

Sometimes, when I bow before the glory of God, singing the doxology at the end of a psalm, I see, from the corner of my eye, as it were, as mirrors reflect into other mirrors, an infinite line of shimmering figures bowing with me.

Or sometimes I will see them *en masse*, as crowds are painted in early Byzantine art. Or sometimes I will see a lone shepherd, or hermit, voice roughened by years of singing against the wind and sun, wandering in his (or her) solitude.

There is a reality to the Communion of Saints that becomes transparently apparent through psalmody, a reality that has a force and power and a "there-ness" which seems more fully manifested in this way than in any other. The music of the psalm-singers, though long silent to the casual ear, lingers in the silence. You can feel it in a church; you can feel it in the ruins of churches in Europe; you can feel it wandering through the mountains wherever shepherds and hermits have lived.

It's more than the knowledge of three thousand years of David's musical heirs; more than the psalms themselves, and the shock of recognition that comes, sometimes, at night, for example, when the sky is so clear you can see stars to the very horizon, and the verse from Psalm 8 echoes continually in your mind: "When I consider your heavens, the work of your fingers; the moon and the stars you have set in their courses, What is man that you should be mindful of him? the son of man that you should seek him out?"

Big Sur is so far from the lights of civilization that you can see the stars not in their usual two-dimensionality, but one behind the other; you have a sense of depth as you look into the heavens, a depth that draws you, an expansive infiniteness, an abyss that opens to eternity, a dark window into the apophatic, pointed with stars, pointed with worlds and universes being born and dying, all rushing toward something at great speed. It has been suggested that all the stars and universes we know are at the outer edge of a black hole, being sucked into it. And we ourselves with them.

And yet having created all of this merely with his "fingers" he is mindful of us; he seeks us out even more than we seek him, and the awe of this overwhelms our senses and not-senses, looking into this dark abyss of the created evidence of Love.

This is one of the links of the divine assembly: knowing that at one time or another in their lives, the psalm-singers each has looked into the heavens and consciously or unconsciously been drawn into this knowledge. The unfathomable, incomprehensible knowledge that the Maker of the starry abyss pursues us through our mortality, exalts us as sons and daughters even in, especially in our mortality, knows us even before we are formed in the womb (Ps 139), knows our longings (Ps 39:9), and whose faithfulness is more than we can ask or imagine or respond to.

So often we tend to think of the psalm-singers (or any other historical—especially biblical—characters) as unreal, as two-dimensional, as paper cutouts, or individuals peopling a drama that is presented and then fades as is its ephemeral nature; at the most the three-dimensionality of a diorama. The best biography gives us only a fantasy picture, and hagiography tends to feed the phantasmagorical.

But to know these men and women also were psalm-singers adds the fourth dimension. They, too, were moved within their depths so as to become mute, so that only psalmody could begin to express the Love at work within, the struggle with darkness, the consuming desire for the Face of God bestowing radiance (Ps 34:5). They, too, wept in frustration at the sparks made manifest for a moment, and then taken away, drawing them deeper and deeper into the apophatic, into the lostness of it all, into the manna-filled desert, dew-fallen music, bread of faithfulness, bread of faith.

They sang, sing, through nights and days, through heat and cold, in deserts and monasteries, leaning in weariness against carved misericords in the night; in skins, in heavy wool, in jeans, in ornate great-schemas, singing, perhaps as I once did with a Trappist friend, Compline on the subway in New York late at night. Except that now there is no night and day for them as they sing; only as in a holograph their time-bound, time-hallowing music is still with us, though we know there is no time; we know there is only motion and bending of space-time. Their density, their holiness, their heart-songs bend with us, bend space-time, bend before the glory of God, with the glory of God, and as we bow before this glory, we, too, add to this density, become mirrored in those mirrors, become massed in those masses—people become Eucharist, one Bread for it all.

JULY

◆

Holocaust

Holocaust

Since the Second World War there has been an increasing number of books published on the events of the holocaust, in which sixty percent of the Jewish population of Europe was exterminated, some six or seven million souls. These books are written by Jews who survived or escaped the concentration camps, by their children, their doctors, and by non-Jews as well.

A former theology professor of mine wrote me a letter in 1978 which read in part, "I gave a talk on my trip this summer to Poland, Russia, Denmark, and Israel with the President's Commission on the Holocaust, along with Elie Wiesel. . . . The impact of Wiesel on me has been very deep, and the issues the holocaust raises for me theologically have to be confronted. I feel an increasing need to reestablish the Jewish roots of the Christian faith, and to find ways to talk about hope and victory in spite of the holocaust, which is a pretty stern negation of any facile Christian triumphalism."

Another letter from a different professor friend also explored this deeply troubling topic: "I am about to go off to the College of the Holy Cross in Worcester to give four days of lectures on 'The Christian Understanding of the Holocaust.' When you have some extra time, try to work that one out! It is now a problem for Christian theology—how do you work out a theodicy in which God appeared to be absent for a long decade, when the forces of the devil were unleashed. That is, of course, if you can believe that 'forces of the devil' are unleashed."

Well, yes, as a matter of fact I can believe in such forces, and they are, from time to time, unleashed. I have only to look within myself to see them. And while I've sought in vain for the "extra time" to ponder the holocaust, it is not the first time I have struggled with it. In fact, there is a part of me, I think, that struggles with it all the time.

In the past, when confronted with unbearable pain and horror, I've taken refuge in Job, who, confronted with the incomprehensibility of the works of God and men, says, "I have spoken of things which I have not understood, things too wonderful for me to know. I knew of thee then only by report, but now I see thee with my own eyes. Therefore I melt away, I repent in dust and ashes."

I don't feel this is a cop-out. But neither is it adequate. To in any way assume that we can understand the interwoven strands of free will, evil, and the redemptive love of God is a presumption.

Once when I was studying Hebrew at a local synagogue, the class became sidetracked by a discussion of Hasidic mysticism, and after I'd expressed a deep respect and appreciation for all that Hasidic writings have meant in my own life (sitting there in my monastic habit), the rabbi asked me in all seriousness why I didn't convert to Judaism.

Stunned, I blurted out the first words that came to my lips: "Because it would be a presumption to deliberately assume that burden of history without being born into it."

I suppose in some ways I've been wrestling with that answer ever since.

The late Bishop C. Kilmer Myers used to tell the story of Emma, a survivor of the holocaust, who regularly at 4 P.M. every day came to stand outside his church on the lower east side of Manhattan and scream imprecations at Jesus. Finally one day, Kim went down to the street and said to Emma, "Why don't you go inside and tell him?" She disappeared into the church. About an hour went by, and Kim, worried, finally went inside, too. He found Emma, prostrate under the rood, absolutely still.

Reaching down, he touched her shoulder. She looked up at him with tears in her eyes and said quietly, "After all, he was a Jew, too."

Elie Wiesel, in his book *Night*, explores the death of his God in the story of the hanging of an "angel-faced" child in the concentration camp in which he, Wiesel, was a prisoner.

"For more than half an hour he stayed there, struggling between life and death, dying in slow agony under our eyes. And we had to look him full in the face. He was still alive when I passed in front of him. His tongue was still red, his eyes were not yet glazed.

"Behind me I heard the same man asking:

" 'Where is God now?'

"And I heard a voice within me answer him:

" 'Where is He? Here He is—He is hanging here on this gallows. . . .' "

The word "holocaust," as generally used in the Old Testament, refers to a burnt whole offering. In ancient Hebrew religion, the holocaust sacrifice was a royal sacrifice, a petitionary sacrifice, made by a king at the beginning of his reign, or before going into battle.

It was also associated with fire from heaven, a sign that the sacrifice being offered was pleasing to God. Thus fire passed through the halves of Abram's sacrifice during his desert wanderings, called as he was out of all that was familiar to go into the Promise; fire fell from heaven to consume Gideon's sacrifice, when he saw the Face of God and did not die; fire fell on David's offering which he made when he saw the angel with the flaming sword. Fire fell on Elijah's offering to mock the priests of Baal, and finally on Elijah himself, with chariots and horses, so completely had his life conformed with the will of God.

One of the most vivid contemporary visual summations of the holocaust was in the first episode of the television series by that name. Only the fire this time fell not from heaven, but was lit of men by the hands of men.

During a pogrom in a Russian village, Jews were herded together and taken to the outskirts of town to their wooden synagogue. There while the men were forced inside, the women were huddled together and made to watch as soldiers spread gasoline around the building and ignited it. As the flames began to leap and crackle, the sound of chanting came from within the building: the men, led by their rabbi, were singing the Kaddish, the prayers for the dead—which include the praise of God—for themselves.

This opening scene for me communicates the essence of a holocaust offering: an incomprehensible whole burnt offering accepted, and, in some mysterious way, assented to by the victims even in the midst of the flames.

I don't pretend to understand this; nor do I pretend to understand the mystery of the whole-offering of our God come to us as a gift and crucified. Yet the two—the twentieth century holocaust and the first century holocaust, and all of the holocausts before and since, are somehow related.

That we will not be able to comprehend this until the consummation of all things is self-evident. And that phrase, the consummation of all things, implies that, at the end of what we call time, all of creation is a sacrifice of praise and thanksgiving to the Alpha and Omega.

The word "consume" itself has association with sacrifice, especially with Eucharist. The Bread is consumed. The Wine is consumed. And each of these elements, even in its ordinary state, is a holocaust. Grain is ground whole and passes through the fire. The wine, too, is a holocaust: in Europe the grape harvest is known as "The Passion of the Grape." The whole fruit is crushed, and in the fermentation process, which generates great amounts of heat, the components of juice-becoming-wine are completely broken down and recombined, the wine pressed out from the grapeskins, and buried in the tomb of a barrel.

And consecrated, we consume these God-given, man-made holocausts, our bodies absorbing them by the same oxidation process, which is fire.

There is a relationship in all this between the offerer and the gift, between priest and sacrifice, that is older than Elijah, older than David, older than Gideon, older than any of the Levitical regulations and definitions. "You shall be my kingdom of priests," says Yahweh in Exodus 19, "my holy nation."

It is the whole nation that is to serve as the chosen mediator, the priest, by which God will reconcile creation to himself, by offering himself.

This relationship of sacrifice and priesthood is highly mutable: the priest becomes part of the sacrifice, part of the holocaust. In Jesus the Christ we see both priest and sacrifice coinhering, becoming interchangeable. In his mystical Body, which is not only the Church but all people to whom blessing and healing are mediated by Israel, the effects of coinherence take on a terrifying aspect.

Is the modern holocaust merely an unleashing of the horrors that dwell within the depths of every human being? I do not know.

Is our growing awareness of the need to "Never forget" the holocaust of that ghastly decade of human history a glimmer of its redemption? I do not know.

Surely these fires were not only "acceptable" in the old language that implies a God in need of appeasement, but he was consumed as well in those ovens? I do not know, but I repent in dust and ashes.

Sacrifice by fire is also sacrifice of praise and thanksgiving. In the twelfth chapter of the Letter to the Hebrews, we are reminded that we stand before "Mount Zion and the city of the living God, heavenly Jerusalem, before myriads of angels, the full concourse and assembly of the firstborn citizens of heaven, and God the judge of all, and the spirits of good men made perfect, and Jesus the mediator of a new covenant, whose sprinkled blood has better things to tell than the blood of Abel. See that you do not refuse to hear the voice that speaks. . . . Let us therefore give thanks to God, and so worship him as he would be worshiped, with reverence and awe; for our God is a consuming fire."

It is *now* that we are standing there; *now* that by our baptism we share in the mediating priesthood of Christ; *now* that Israel and the New Israel are mediators of blessing and healing to all creation. And yet, the same chapter reminds us "not to lose heart and grow faint. In your struggle against sin you have not yet resisted to the point of shedding your blood."

Most commentaries say that this passage refers to martyrdom in the arena. But it also brings to mind the agony in the Garden of Gethsemani, the agony of which our lives are a reflection as we attempt to listen to the voice that speaks, to wrestle against our desire to pander to our own egos, our selfish appetites, our laziness and apathy, and the potential horrors that lurk in our depths, the warfare in which all of us without exception are engaged in our Christian vocation.

Today in our uneasy culture of casual brutality, nuclear intimidation, and the cheapness of life, we are constantly faced with outward and visible signs of an immense inward and spiritual grace, a gift of the Holy Spirit, which is to *let go*. The various processes of letting go can also be thought of as holocaust, of letting go of the familiar and therefore safe concepts of self, of how things ought to be and never will, of how they have been— so we can bring about the genuinely new order, which is the only means by which the earth will survive; of going out, like Abram, from all that is familiar, from the illusion of security into the desert where fire falls from heaven.

For all our world has become this desert. Here, in our wanderings, we are called to make each place, like Little Gidding, a place where prayer can be valid. And then to let it go; to make each step, each moment, a holocaust of prayer, praise, and thanksgiving, and then let it go. And this letting go is itself the heart of prayer: the cry of the heart that has emptied itself of everything that is most precious to it—even its own idea of itself— so that it may be filled with the fire of the living God.

We are all journeying into the wilderness in faith, and we are all, though it may remain completely hidden, given one of the greatest gifts God gives of himself: the gift of Abraham: to go into the Promise, into the vows we have made by our baptism, knowing we are called out of all that is familiar, to bless God for it, to bless the unknown, to bless, finally, even our own death.

The future is always unknown, but in these latter days there are no longer even any inklings of what will be asked of us, whether city-dweller or woodland hermit. One thing only is sure: that we will be asked to accept, thank, offer and repent in the midst of constant flux.

In Rite I of the 1979 Book of Common Prayer, there is a clause that is comprehensible only in a Eucharistic context: "And here we offer and present unto thee, O Lord, our selves, our souls and bodies, to be a reasonable, holy, and living sacrifice unto thee. . . ."

It bears close examination. In the eyes of the world there is nothing reasonable about such an act; in our own eyes, judging from our history and our propensities, there is nothing holy about us, and a holocaust, a whole burnt sacrifice, implies our death.

Yet these selves of ours are touched with fire from heaven, and we begin to understand that what is unreasonable is that what we have to offer is so little; that what is given is holy because it is returning to God, fragmented and charred to be sure, what he has made to delight in; and living, because we have passed with him through death into life everlasting.

We often think of Eucharist as bringing the eternal into time. But perhaps it is more fruitful to think of Eucharist—which can be made, by the priesthood of our baptism, in each moment of time—as gathering the temporal into the eternal.

In this incarnate, sacramental glimpse out of time into God's no-time, contemporary astrophysics makes it a little easier than in the past to look at this mystery by analogy. We can liken it to being drawn, as it were, into a black hole, a collapsed star, where everything becomes compressed and intensified. A black hole is not a point, but an infinitely mutable event, drawing all matter that comes within its gravitational influence into itself. And passing through the singularity, the "wormhole" or timewarp where all laws break down, that connects the black hole with its opposite counterpart, we are expelled through the white hole, which is infinitely expanding.

Because we are drawn to the holocaust, to the Host, and we are changed not only by the consecrated Bread and Wine, but also by each other, by the lives and deaths around us, by the lives and deaths in our own lives, not only major dislocations and new beginnings, but also the small deaths, our destruction of each other and forgiving of each other. And having passed through his death, resurrection, we are expelled into the world, redeeming by God's infinitely expanding love.

But for all the inexorability, the choices still have to be made: to change and grow, or not to change, to listen to the fantasies that ravel deeper into anger, resentment, and hate; or to struggle to adore, to face through the phantasms of our own evil that would prevent our offering, prevent sacrifice; to persist, until our own personal solitude becomes an intensification of the world of cruelty, hunger, poverty, and despair; an Israel, struggling, wrestling with the God whom we will not let go and who will not let us go, until we become an intensification of the world's healing, blessing, and joy.

We are victims of mercy.

Catherine of Siena puts it this way: "Just as in the Old Testament when sacrifice was offered to God, a fire came and drew to himself the sacrifice that was acceptable to him, so gentle Truth did that to the soul. He sent the fiery mercy of the Holy Spirit and seized the sacrifice of desire that she had made of herself to him."

A priest friend put all of this into simpler language for me: "If you make your vows, and try hard to keep them, and are truly sorry when you don't, and inflict as little pain and suffering on others as possible, at the last day our Lord will give you a crown of glory that will never fade away. What more could you ask for than that?"

How do I understand holocaust, any holocaust? I don't. I hope to spend the rest of my life in the exploration of the aweful knowledge of man as both priest and sacrifice, persecutor and victim, executioner and redeemer.

With Francois Mauriac in his introduction to Wiesel's *Night*, the language of my response dissolves into the silence of weeping:

> And I, who believe that God is love, what answers could I give
> my young questioner, whose dark eyes still held the reflection
> of that angelic sadness which had appeared one day upon the
> face of the hanged child? What did I say to him? Did I speak of
> that other Israeli, his brother who may have resembled him—
> the Crucified, whose Cross has conquered the world? Did I af-
> firm that the stumbling block to his faith was the cornerstone
> of mine, and the conformity between the Cross and the suffer-
> ing of men was in my eyes the key to that impenetrable mys-
> tery whereon the faith of his childhood had perished? ... We
> do not know the worth of one single drop of blood, one single
> tear. All is grace. If the Eternal is the Eternal, the last word

for each one of us belongs to Him. This is what I should have told this Jewish child. But I could only embrace him, weeping.

Thus, having uttered what I do not understand, things too wonderful for me; now in the hope of seeing God with my own eyes, I melt away; I become one with these ashes, and repent.

Lord, make us holocaust for your people,
    pure channels for your love;
    send your Holy Spirit to enflame our hearts,
    and receive us into the fire of your life,
    O blessed Trinity,
    Father, Son, and Holy Spirit
    who live and reign in glory everlasting.
    Amen.

AUGUST

◆

Big Sur Diptych II
Vigil of the Transfiguration

Star Fox

On the way to the waterpipe yesterday evening saw a lynx; he saw me, too, and slunk quickly off to the left side of the road, where a grocery store of quail and woodrats awaited his leisurely selection in the brush.

Filled my jugs and heard a crashing in the woods above; deer from the sound of it. I went a little up the road, set my jugs down to rest, and watched, and waited. The crashing resumed. A doe appeared, slipped noisily down to the road and began to eat, seemingly indifferent to surroundings, but checking things out for her fawn.

Fawn is impatient: leaps lightly down to the road, frisking. His back is to me, but suddenly the doe sees me and watches with dark eyes, ears twitching. I am upwind of her, so I know she has my scent, yet she seems unafraid. After a moment she leans down for another mouthful, and I quietly pick up my jugs to leave these two in peace. They watch me but do not leave, do not panic. I am blessed.

Four A.M., and a broad-bottomed 'coon wakes me up, raiding my stores. I shine my light on him, and he scuttles off into the bushes; soon comes back. I chunk a clod of dirt after him and wait under the wheeling bowl of stars to see if he will return again.

A meteor shoots overhead. We are in the time of major star showers during the year. This one is bright and yellow and goes from east to west.

And suddenly I see the fox, also moving from east to west. I hold my breath: he trails stars from his tail as he floats along, seeming to walk a few inches above the earth, mincing, dancing over the dry grass, hardly making a sound, no sound that I can hear.

He pauses, dances even in his stillness. He calls down Aries, the warrior, and tames him: no war, only music and fire. He calls down the great star Aldebaran from the constellation of the bull (how well I know the bull!) and the fire strikes the earth. He laughs with the Pleiades, those shy maidens whom you can see only if you look at them out of the corner of your eye: look at them directly, and they seem to recede; yet look at them through binoculars, and they stand out brighter than Aldebaran, even the shyest.

Fox, little fox, there are no sour grapes or sweet for you here, only light, starlight, stars' dust, clouds of unknowing, only to you they are known. It is we with our names and intuitions who must grope; you flicker down from the heavenly spheres and bring with you the whole population of the universe; centaur and scorpion; warrior and maiden; hunter and starry game. But there is no plunder of centaurs; no sting of scorpions; no carrying off of maiden by warrior; no consuming of game by hunter.

You carry us, little fox, into this assembly; you make us seek him who made the Pleiades and Orion, you carry them to us, us to them; we wheel and dance; we plunge into the darkness and are dazzled with the light. We know deep darkness becomes morning, and wonder at the brightness of the stars as first light's sheer and gauzy veil is cast over the eastern ridge of the mountains.

Star fox, little swift, trailing starlight and constellations behind you, forgive our heaviness, forgive our clay feet. Tell our Maker that we too would dance in the darkness and in the desert; tell him we would have your lightness and grace; tell him, O little one of large eyes and huge ears, that we would see him and hear his voice; tell him for us: our words are so clumsy, our hearing so dulled.

Tell him: for he knows we are dancers, singers; we trail fire in our hearts as we hurtle through space-time. Your eyes glow in the starlight, and you look into our hearts and know this;

your ears move receptively, and you hear our pleas, know our longing, as does he.

But tonight; this moonless night of music and ever-changing, never-changing dance, speak for us, hear for us, dance for us, bring us into the starry company; bring them to us.

Lightning in the East

I awake from sodden sleep. Drugged with dreams from Bosch that sneak into the bushes as consciousness makes a half-hearted return.

The night is getting warm: I went to bed in a flannel night-gown; it and my sleeping bag are soaked with sweat.

My left sinus hurts. Hurts with an ache that is sharp and dull and full at once, a sure sign of changing pressure.

Change. Something is about to happen.

I struggle out of my damp cocoon and zip open the tent door.

Twenty-three hundred feet below me, muffling the surf, glimmering in the moonless night, is a bed of fog. Silly with sleep, I think for a moment of making a swan-dive off my mountain perch and bouncing on it.

Then I wake up fast. There is lightning in the east. It dulls the stars as it explodes, and then makes them seem all the brighter when it is gone. I sense, rather than hear, the rumble of thunder. It comes through the rock in the mountains that stir uneasily with the pressure that at once both rises and falls. The water in their heart is summoned by the water from heaven falling in torrents into the valley to the southeast.

The stars seem caught in their motion, motionless. The temperature rises. The fog rises a little, too. It is both hotter and colder. Somewhere on this mountain, heat and cold will meet; somewhere on this mountain, fire and water.

I am caught and cower. The earth trembles toward the dawn as lightning shows the ridges in sharp relief. All is hushed in this waiting, all exhausted in the tension. Little by little the fog creeps up the mountain. Sharper and brighter the lightning flashes to the east.

Cry to the mountains, "Fall on us!" and to the hills, "Hide us!" Who can bear this tearing polarity; who can be the arc between fire and water, rock and bread, tears and wine? Who can stand a heart riven by the darkling light; who can bear the molten Love coursing through the earth?

There is a line of fire that stretches from heaven to meet the line of fog rising from the sea. What will be released in this elemental meeting; what energy from polarity, what mutation from their collision?

I am caught halfway up, halfway down the mountain; I am caught between heaven and earth; I am caught by the fire that speaks to fire indwelling, and the water that calls to my tears. I arc to meet the lightning and embrace the mercy of fog to cool my burns.

Star Fox and Red Bull swirl in the Dance; Psalm-singers in voices without number charge the silence with music no mortal ear can hear and live. The lines of fog and fire draw closer.

What is man, O Lord, that you are mindful of him? What is man that you should make him a meeting place of these contraries, torn between earth and heaven? What is man that through him fire should erupt from creation, and cleanse all things, that Beauty should return in her fullness, that star should marry sea, and Peace kiss each one upon the lips?

The stars bend low. "Tonight?" I ask, longing through my fear; is it tonight? Star and fire and fog blend together; the weight is too much to bear, and weighs nothing . . . and then . . . and then . . .

A little breeze rustles through the dried husks of wild oats, whose seed has long since fallen into the ground to wait for winter rains. Its sighing is my longing; the husks my food until I return to the Father . . . grain planted in me and ground and leavened and broken.

Sunrise dulls the stars; lightning fades; fog recedes. Star Fox and Red Bull sleep until the Feast of feasts. And yet . . . and yet . . .

The Fire of Your Life

How is the sorrowing earth not transfigured this night? How is this sowing of fire in all things not sparked, arced through our clay this night, this morning, this darkness and light both alike?

Time is our foolish booth in which we try to trap what has begun and ended and even now is borne in us. We are blinded because we see, but it is in the cloud that envelops us and leaves us senseless that we know a little the Truth of it all, dimly, stupidly, and return home rejoicing, not believing, hoping it is as we knew, and yet not, because it is beyond our knowing.

The sun burns its way into the morning, burns our staring eyes, burns us into new life of another day. We break bread at sun's zenith, cry, "O Christ, come quickly, Lord!" Under sun beg for Sun; broken-hearted fed with Bread broken, hearts pierced with light too great to bear, burst asunder with all creation pouring out of each in flood-life of him, fountains, streams, rivers from stoneheartflesh, molten, living stones.

SEPTEMBER
◆
Intercession

Intercession

O Lord, open our eyes to see you;
open our ears to hear you;
open our hearts to know you;
we beg through Jesus Christ our Lord. Amen.

I'm fascinated by the ways in which people approach intercession.

The Anglican Communion, for example, has a regular cycle of prayer for the Church in the world.

Then there are people who keep elaborate notebooks crammed with names. Catherine Doherty tells us she keeps a notebook beneath an icon of our Lady, and she is sure the Blessed Virgin reads that book to her Son at night.

One day I visited Washington Cathedral in the company of a seven-year-old boy, who asked what the rack of candles in the Chapel of the Holy Spirit was all about. I told him, and helped him light one for a prayer of his own.

A Trappist abbot I know has a huge poster of Our Lady of Guadalupe in his office, and underneath is a sort of cup where he puts slips of paper with names and intentions.

C.S. Lewis tells us in *Letters to Malcolm* that he usually asks God to care for "the lady on the train," or "the old crock in the greengrocer's," or something like that. But God understands.

The other day I read that Carthusians use no names at all because, the author rather nastily remarked, they don't want to ruin the purity of their prayer. Well, the Carthusians may be on to something, but I suspect the man who wrote that doesn't understand what he is seeing, any more than the tourists in the Syrian and Egyptian deserts understood what they saw, and twisted and distorted the meaning of the lives of the solitaries into an ancient *Guinness Book of Records,* instead of discerning their struggle for purity of heart as the transforming of ordinary lives by the power of God.

Now, just as it is folly to say, "Notebook-keepers are better than Carthusians," or, "This technique of prayer is better than that," or to try to judge or evaluate our prayer, saying, "This was a good prayer," or, "This was a higher form of prayer," so it is equally foolish to impose some artificial form of intercession on ourselves just because it seems the right thing to do.

Yet I think we have to ask the question: What is it we do when we intercede?

First of all, I think we have to realize that we're not always at the top of our form, and so we have to pray what we are able to pray. Sometimes this can be very Old Testament, very primitive.

When I was living in Manhattan some years ago, and, for reasons I won't go into, had spent some time trying to kill the prayer that kept rising in me like an unwanted gas bubble in a twenty-loaf blob of bread dough, I finally came to realize that my efforts to push this bubble down and deny its existence were futile, and, very frightened of being overwhelmed if I stopped fighting it, asked a friend what I should do.

"Oh," he said, "pray for things like taxicabs when you need them. If it makes you feel safer, don't ask God for them, but pray to something inanimate like a fire hydrant."

So I spent the next few weeks experimenting with this idea, and whenever I was late for an appointment, I prayed to the nearest fire hydrant for a cab.

It was amazing.

Taxis would appear from nowhere. If ten people along the block were signaling for cabs, the one that appeared would stop in front of me. I could get taxis at rush hour. I could get taxis in the rain. I could get taxis at rush hour in the rain on the Friday of a three-day weekend!

By the time God decided this joke had gone on long enough and sent me the Dark Night of the Taxicab, I was still just as frightened, but at the same time a little more ready to let go my illusory control over prayer. (I might add that I've never been able to get taxis in New York since!)

We have to pray where we are, and what we can. And we shouldn't try to fool ourselves; intercession is hard work. We are lazy about it and avoid it for very good reasons. Prayer, especially intercession, is warfare. Prayer is death. As we pray we fast; as we pray we die: we have to deny ourselves everything else that is in our lives and just *do* it.

And what are we doing when we intercede? Often, in our heart of hearts, we seem to be trying to manipulate God, asking him to change his mind. The ancient Romans used the word "intercede" to mean, "interposing a veto." We often seem to be trying to veto God, standing over and against him, wheedling him, bargaining with him. This is the pagan Old Testament God, not the God of Sinai, rooted in the stable gift of the Law. This is the capricious deity who needs to be pleased and placated, not the loving New Testament God, whose wisdom and judgment are given from the perspective of crucifixion and resurrection.

This false stereotype of the Old Testament God is very prevalent, perhaps because, like the fire hydrant, it is safe. We know what we're dealing with. If we can confine God to our own categories, our own safe boundaries and concepts, he won't ask too much of us; we won't be overwhelmed.

Now, I don't think God rejects this sort of prayer; in fact, I don't think he rejects any prayer. His acceptance of our prayer can perhaps be illustrated by the story of the two men who jointly owned a car and had to suffer through parking it in Manhattan where, because of street cleaning, they had to play musical parking places each morning and night.

Finally, fed up with the hassle, one man suggested to the other that they make a phony sale of the car to a friend in New Jersey. Then, with New Jersey plates, they could get away with not having to move it each day; there would not be as great a risk of getting ticketed or towed. But the second man asked, "What would God say?" To which the first replied, "If God had a car and had to park it in Manhattan, he'd understand."

God understands. And when I catch myself in this particular Old Testament attitude of intercession, I imagine that I also catch a glimmer of divine amusement.

But intercessory prayer is *not* safe, not if we choose to enter into it in a deeper way. Intercession, like all other kinds of prayer, is really a form of adoration, and the farther we move into it, the more likely we are to forget ourselves, our ideas, our desires, in the Face of this light and love.

What we cannot understand in terms of pain and suffering is often an invitation to enlarge our hearts. Lately the image of the lady with the alabaster box has been much in my mind. We are the lady, and our hearts are made of stone. When they are opened, God pours his love through us onto his Body, which is each other.

Sometimes, of course, through fear or rage or other sin, that box snaps shut—maybe on our fingers—and we are left there struggling to find the key that will open it again. And, paradoxically, that key can often be intercession: the access to Love is love, or, to put it another way, when we feel incapable of entering into the pure Love of God, we can make ourselves available to it by natural love, by holding someone dear to us in him.

Anthony Bloom describes this process in *Courage To Pray*. He is referring to the late Staretz Silouan of Mount Athos. "Let us be encouraged," Bloom writes, "by the story of the monk who was praying for his neighbors and who gradually lost consciousness of this earth because he became so wrapped up in God, and who found all his neighbors again in God."

Often we pray for people by their given names, but, like C.S. Lewis, I'm forgetful of names, and I, too, refer God to "the man in the hardware store," or, "the child feeding the swans." But, again, God understands. The name *he* hears is not the given human name in any case, but rather the secret name with which he has named—brought into being—the person we're praying for, the name written on the white stone to be given each of us at the parousia.

Do we dare to enter into the bringing-into-being of another? And conversely, do we dare to ask a friend, or the saints, to enter into our bringing-into-being? Do we dare ask God to pray the saints for us, to allow them to share with us himself, poured out through their own particular brokenness by which his Word is spread abroad in our world? It's a terrifying prospect.

But this is the priestly vocation of our baptism: to be mediators of reconciliation, dispensers, vehicles for the love of God.

There is a gadget in communications satellites called a transponder. Its purpose is to focus and intensify signals as it passes them on. And to make ourselves available for this entering into another's being is to enter the darkness of the unknown.

But there is a problem with this image because we are changed by what we pray, as the transponder is not. We run the risk of being burnt up, of being holocaust for each other.

Sometimes this is evidenced when suddenly there is an awareness in prayer, visualized or not, of actually being with the person prayed for: walking down the street with a friend or stranger; watching a surgical procedure and at the same time being on the table, sustaining the other's breath with your own; sitting in a small, dim room with someone near despair; holding a sick child in your arms.

When the American Airlines DC 10 crashed at O'Hare in the spring of 1979, such an experience came, unbidden, as I sat down for evening meditation. As prayer for those people pushed aside all else, there was a vivid sense of being in the plane's cabin among them in their agony and horror as they were falling toward the earth. This was repeated over and over during the next half-hour, as if the prayer itself required my enduring those terrible moments.

This is the intercession of entering in, and while we can choose or choose not to make this sort of thing part of our prayer, it also comes to us un-looked for, sometimes frighteningly so.

Charles Williams in *Descent into Hell* describes this entering in as the doctrine of substituted love. Stanhope, who is making the choice, is talking to a girl who keeps meeting a doppelganger, a vision of herself. She is very afraid.

> "To bear a burden is precisely to carry it instead of," said Stanhope. "If you're still carrying yours, I'm not carrying it for you—however sympathetic I may be. And anyhow, there's

no need to introduce Christ, unless you wish. It's a fact of experience. If you give a weight to me, you can't be carrying it yourself; all I'm asking you to do is to notice that blazing truth. It doesn't sound very difficult."

"And if I could," she said. "If I could do—whatever it is you mean, would I? Would I push my burden on to anybody else?"

"Not if you insist on making a universe for yourself," he answered. "If you want to disobey and refuse the laws that are common to us all, if you want to live in pride and division and anger, you can. But if you will be part of the best of us, and laugh and be ashamed with us, then you must carry someone else's burden. I haven't made the universe, and it isn't my fault. But I'm sure that this is a law of the universe, and not to give up your parcel is quite as much to rebel as not to carry another's. You'll find it quite easy if you let yourself do it."

Then Stanhope gives the girl his instructions.

"When you are alone," he said, "remember that I am afraid instead of you, and that I have taken over every kind of worry. Think merely that; say to yourself—'he is being worried,' and go on. Remember it is mine. If you do not see it, well; if you do, you will not be afraid . . . because you will leave all that to me."

Then there is the intercession of actual substitution—the offering of oneself instead of—which is, if you stop to think about it, probably the most appalling form of intercessory prayer. It is definitely the response to a call, an invitation, and not lightly undertaken. Bloom describes such a substitution in a concrete encounter between two women during the Russian civil war.

In a small provincial village which had just changed hands, a young woman of twenty-seven or so was trapped with her two small children. Her husband belonged to the opposite side. She had been unable to escape in time, and she was in hiding, trying to save her own and her children's lives. She spent a

day and a night in great fear and the following evening the
door of her hiding place was opened and a young woman, a
neighbour of her own age, came in. She was a simple woman
with nothing extraordinary about her. She said, "Is So and So
your name?" The mother replied, "Yes," in great fear. The
neighbor said, "You have been discovered; they are coming for
you tonight to shoot you. You must leave." The mother looked
at her children and said, "Where shall I go? How can I get
away with these children. They could not walk fast enough or
far enough for us not to be caught." And this neighbour suddenly became a neighbour in the full sense of the gospel. She
approached the mother and said with a smile, "They will not
go after you, because I will stay here in your place." The
mother must have said, "They will shoot you." She replied,
"Yes, but I have no children. You *must* leave." And the mother
went.

Substitution can also occur in the realm of pure prayer, but
here in this mystery we must yield entirely to the love of Christ
praying us in ways far beyond our knowing.

There is no way to judge and evaluate intercession. God
knows the secrets of our hearts and does most of his work in and
through us when we are least aware of it, when our prayer
seems most useless and insipid, or when we're not aware of
praying at all.

Sometimes we are allowed a glimpse, or given some kind of
reassurance, but this is rare. God is wise to give us dry rations
because he knows that in our frailty we would quickly begin to
pray for consolations for ourselves, instead of breaking out of
our inhibitions and away from our safe fire hydrants to participate in his love for others.

It is this participation that Saint Paul refers to in his Letter
to the Colossians when he speaks of making up what is lacking
in the sufferings of Christ: that, though Christ has triumphed,
he asks us to struggle with him, in his love in the battles still
raging with the cosmic powers of darkness.

So, whether you intercede like a notebook-keeper, or like a
Carthusian, be aware that you are leaving yourself wide open to
be used in some unknowable way. And if you are feeling that

you've been forgotten, left out, or unheard, do not give up, for God has sent out his Light and his Truth, who is leading us to his holy hill and to his dwelling.

> *Glory to God whose power working in us can do infinitely more than we can ask or imagine; glory to him from generation to generation in the Church and in Christ Jesus for ever and ever.*

OCTOBER

◆

All Hallows Eve

All Hallows Eve

Once on a cool September evening, I put on my sweater and sandals, flicked on the porch lamp, and went outside into the moist autumn air to go to a Eucharist at the chapel across the way. My eyes adjusted enough to see the hermitage's wooden steps, but beyond the edges of light were shadows, and I had to trust to the memory of my feet for the stone flight going up the hill.

As I stepped out into the dark, there was a tearing shriek, a noise like rubbing your wet hand over the surface of a tightly blown-up balloon, or like tires' friction on the road when you jam on the brakes.

I looked down and saw a half-dead bluejay, one of the cats' offerings, bloody evidence of a hope that the gift of this delicate morsel would convince me I should relent and allow the donor to become the official hermit cat.

Ugh.

My one hundred and forty pounds had squeezed a column of air out of the bird's four-ounce body through its constricted throat. That was what made the noise. Though I doubt the bird still could have been alive, its body, under my gaze, stirred with faint neurological twitchings. I quickly dispatched it, threw it out into the blackness toward the leaf-pit, and, with a kind of hollow helplessness in my stomach, made my way over to chapel for the Eucharist.

During the liturgy the question revolved continually in my mind: Why, why by our very existence, must we involuntarily damage others? It's bad enough to have the capacity for willful sin. And at the Offertory was all the groaning and travail of creation.

I have been haunted by this question for many years, not only in terms of the natural order, but also in the relationships of human beings with one another. I will never forget the day when I first understood what the old spiritual writers call "instant mutual antipathy," that there are people in this world who will damage me and whom I will damage simply by existing, without doing anything, but merely being.

For some people, to be intimidating is to live with an exhilarating sense of power, but for me, in every encounter of this nature, I experience deep shame, humiliation, pain, self-loathing, and grief.

This fact of human relationships, I have come to believe, lies at the root of what we call original sin, and which we tend to shrug off as something we can't do particularly much about.

Often when we talk about the Fall we speak in nervously jocular terms, like the end man in a minstrel show, retelling the story of the snake who gave Eve the apple, who ate and gave to Adam to eat, and when the Lord God walked in the garden in the cool of the evening, and asked Adam where he was and what he had done, Adam pointed to Eve, Eve pointed to 'de snake, and 'de snake, he lay low.

This reading from Genesis frequently inspires uneasy laughter, a laughter that flies in the face of phantasms flickering at the edge of our vision, and a pervasive miasma of evil that penetrates our defenses and tries to influence our every choice.

This is the season of ghoulies and ghosties, long leggety

beasties, and things that go bump in the night, the season when we trivialize the horror of the vaguely known, or, worse, try by psychologizing to dismiss the ghastly propensities that live in the depths of our own hearts, biding their time, waiting for their chance.

Maybe we try to tell ourselves that this is the only season of the year when familiars emerge, and that, for one night, we can let them out to play without too much risk, knowing that the bells heralding the morning of saints and souls will drive these wraiths back underground, much like Disney's vision of the night on Bald Mountain.

Oh no.

Oh no.

This is the delusion that the Evil One would have us take as truth: that he doesn't really exist, that he is a neurosis, or a bad case of indigestion, or a child's night-terror.

You may scoff. You may ask with a note of incredulity: Do you really believe that old stuff?

And I will feel the dread in my heart and say:

Oh yes.

Oh yes.

I believe.

And perhaps you will say with an amused, knowing look: But how? Why?

And I will say: I know. I have seen him. I have heard his cajoling. I have felt his creeping, paralyzing presence.

And you will look at me as if I am quite mad.

And perhaps I am.

But I have seen him: I have seen him in the face of hate of a Vietnamese officer executing a Viet Cong prisoner at point blank range four feet in front of a news photographer. I have seen him in the face of my older sister in one of our ancient sibling rages.

I have looked in the mirror and seen him in my own face.

I have heard his voice whisper, "Just this once," or, "No one will know," or, "Self-discipline can be harmful to your psychological health."

I have seen him waiting by my bed as racing, angry, obsessive thoughts wrestle in my consciousness with the Jesus Prayer. And he waits, waits for me to make my choice.

Oh yes. I know him well.

And yet within that opportunity for choice lies my hope of salvation.

It is no accident that we shutter our houses against principalities and powers on the night before we celebrate those saints and souls who have endured this warfare in themselves, and died reaching for the Light they glimpsed oblique and veiled, that now burst in full radiance upon them.

We make heroes of them, and indeed they were. We magnify their deeds, and they were great deeds.

But if we look beyond the fabulous that has obscured the humanity of the saints, we see that their heroism was the heroism of ordinary life, and that their deeds sprang from the miracle of the redemptive love of God in Christ Jesus, from which all the demons of the universe, all the cosmic powers of evil, could not separate them.

We have lost our sense of Incarnation. We have debased it to something magical. We have obscured the elemental quality of Sacrament, stable-born and crucified, and locked him away in golden tabernacles.

We need to recover the elemental. We need to acknowledge the warfare. We need to see redemption at work in the most fundamental laws of the universe.

I will never forget the day one summer when one of the friars came home to the friary where I had my hermitage. He jumped out of the borrowed yellow VW bug, and, catching sight of me, joyfully shouted, "Did you see in the New York *Times* that the Second Law of Thermodynamics has been repealed?"

Yes, I had seen it, and responded with equal joy.

The Second Law of Thermodynamics had been the scientific refutation of resurrection, the spiritual and cultural depressant of our age. It was the law of entropy. It said, in essence, that everything in the universe proceeded surely and inexorably toward destruction and decay.

But someone in Europe discovered that out of disintegrating particles come new and more subtly complex forms, that very rottenness spawns new life.

And since the functioning of particles ultimately is expressed in the functioning of larger forms like plants and birds and cats and humans, planets and galaxies, black holes and universes, the announcement in the *Times* has vast implications of hope, the sort of hope that makes us doubtful Christians look at each other in relief and say bravely, "I told you so."

Now, you may ask, what does this arcane law of particle physics have to do with ghoulies and ghosties, with Sacrament and saints?

Simply this: that embracing the incomprehensible pain of fang and claw, guarding the shades of the Evil One, transforming the deadly propensities dwelling in us is a Love that enfolds pain, casts down Evil, and purifies our hearts.

That far from understanding creation as having fallen once for all, it is still falling, just as it is still being redeemed.

Prayer can be participating in another's bringing-into-being. But this participation is not confined to intercession: it is the prayer of our enduring what lives within and around us, the prayer of our very lives that, at every moment, we can choose to participate in the bringing-into-being of more evil, or the bringing-into-being of that Kingdom where there is no more pain or death, and where God through his own suffering in Jesus who is the Christ wipes away every tear from every eye.

And where we shall see him face to Face.

"He who gives this testimony speaks, 'Yes, I am coming soon!' "

Amen. Even so, Maranatha, come quickly, Lord Jesus!

NOVEMBER

◆

Kontakion

Kontakion

The sons of the prophets who were at Jericho drew near to Elisha, and said to him, "Do you know that today the Lord will take away your master from over you?" And he answered, "Yes, I know it; hold your peace."

Then Elijah said to him, "Tarry here, I pray you; for the Lord has sent me to the Jordan." But he said, "As the Lord lives and as you yourself live, I will not leave you." . . . Then Elijah took his mantle, and rolled it up, and struck the water, and the water was parted to the one side and to the other, till the two of them could go over on dry ground.

When they had crossed, Elijah said to Elisha, "Ask what I shall do for you before I am taken from you." And Elisha said, "I pray you, let me inherit a double share of your spirit." And he said, "You have asked a hard thing; yet, if you see me as I am being taken from you, it shall be so for you; but if you do not see me, it shall not be so." And as they still went on and talked, behold, a chariot of fire and horses of fire separated the two of them. And Elijah went up by a whirlwind into heaven. And Elisha saw it and he cried, "My father, my father! the chariots of Israel and its horsemen!" And he saw him no more.

Then he took hold of his own clothes and rent them in two pieces. And he took up the mantle of Elijah that had fallen from him, and went back and stood on the bank of the Jordan. Then he took the mantle of Elijah that had fallen from him, and struck the water, saying, "Where is the Lord, the God of Elijah?" And when he had struck the water, the water was parted to the one side and to the other; and Elisha went over.

2 Kings 2:5-6, 8-14 RSV (Common Bible)

When the Franciscan friar who was very much a spiritual father to me died, he left me, along with his other spiritual sons and daughters, a portion of his mantle. And after his death, for some weeks and months, like Elisha I lashed the water with his mantle and called on his God. I did a lot of growing up.

We seem to grow at different rates. Each of us has his or her own rhythm. And within each of us are different rhythms: our bodies grow at one rate, our psyches at another, our souls at yet another, or so it seems. It is all really one fabric being woven, woven by a master Weaver who, like the artist he is, knows that the most beautiful are those in which the flaws and mistakes and gaps are left, integrated into the finished work.

Our bodies grow comparatively rapidly. By the time we are twenty or so, it's all complete, as complete as it will ever be. And from the age of twenty-five, so we are told, physically it's all downhill.

Our psyches and particularly our souls are a different matter. By twenty our psyches have just begun to cope with the unimaginably vast amounts of conscious and unconscious material that have been put into our own particular stew, mixed with the unique genetic material each of us is given.

Most of us come out of adolescence with a burning energy expressed partly as unfocused anger or rage, partly as the creative drive that will focus our lives into some sort of coherent whole, partly as a deep unconscious groping that will keep us searching to the end for the God who is both so close and familiar, and yet so far beyond our knowing.

I had a friend, a lady, one of the last of the great ladies in the old manner. She had been crippled by arthritis for nearly twenty years, but remained indomitable. Only in the last few years of her life did she slow down a little, not being able, for example, to manage shipboard travel any longer, but still solicitous of her husband's every childish whim.

He, at ninety-one, had never grown up. Having come from a Prussian family where there was a nanny to tie his shoes, he saw no reason to learn to do that, though he mastered the intricacies of the stock market at an early age.

There are different ways of being a child.

This friend of mine, who was herself nearing her nineties, confided to me once on a mellow evening, "Don't be fooled, dearie. It's only our bodies that grow old, and inside I'm still a young girl who dances until dawn."

Wisdom, wisdom born of love and suffering, is a gift that comes from and with the God we seek. My spiritual father had that wisdom; others who have been spiritual parents to me have it. But if you mentioned it to any of these people they would look at you with irony, knowing theirs is but a fragment, or not aware of it at all.

Growing up is hard.

For us late bloomers it takes most of our twenties for grief over our hubris and callowness to burn most of the rage out of us and make us painfully aware of how careful we must be. We go from feeling that we are not listened to or paid attention to realizing the tremendous, sometimes terrifying impact that our words, actions, and, yes, our prayer, have on others.

The beginning, gnawing knowledge of just who we really are and of the price of our forgiveness ceases being a source of rebellion and becomes a welcome, burning fire, a fire that sears and purifies, and yet does not consume.

So much of growing up is letting go: letting go our ideas of what life should be like, for instance. It often takes a long time and to let go the conviction that life is or ought to be fair and satisfying according to our youthful concepts. That's part of the rage. And the way that rage is grieved out is through knowledge that life will never be fair, or ever the way we expect. This is knowledge that comes through disappointment, through loss, through our being broken again and again.

After the death of my Franciscan father, my childhood, especially my spiritual childhood, seemed to melt away like patches of snow under a heavy rain.

One of the hardest things about growing up is that you suddenly find that your parents are your children. This happened to me some years before the Franciscan's death. It's a shock. You realize that your parents are looking to *you* for solace, for nurturing, and in spite of the illusion you help them to maintain that they are still in charge, each of you knows with the certainty born of long association that the shoe is on the other foot, that the worm has turned.

This is an unrecoverable loss, and worth grieving over. But it takes a while. You go through a lot of waste motion testing this new, unsure, sometimes swampy ground to deal with your sadness and disbelief. And then one day something happens, or maybe it isn't even that specific, and the reality of the situation settles in. It's a whole new ballgame. (There is always, of course, the sudden re-reversal of roles, and the wisdom and love that remain—they are still your *parents*. But that's another subject.)

And I suppose when one's parents die, an experience I have yet to have, the feeling of being out there without any walls or sure touch-points except the invisible cradling hand of God is impressed upon you with even more force.

I'm beginning to think that this reversal of roles is even more poignant with one's spiritual parents. When my Franciscan father learned of his illness, our roles subtly began to reverse themselves. Since we had first talked at the beginning of our fourteen-year relationship, we had often spoken of death as the only passage to seeing the loving Face of God, which is the terrible longing that brings us to the religious life in the first place, and that, with seeming paradox (and we agreed that paradox is illusion), makes every moment of life all the more precious.

A year or so before he knew of his final illness, this friar spoke with some amusement of the years he had spent railing at God because he would not take him to himself sooner—and then, with a little embarrassment at the folly of this, of his resignation to take it at God's pace.

Then he found out he was ill. And when he first wrote me that he was to die, I wrote back, "When you go home for Christmas"—for this was the image his own death brought to his mind—"ask our blessed Lord not to make me wait too long."

I don't think he ever stopped being impatient with God. And so, when I said what I knew would be our final goodbye, as we stood after he blessed me, I gently teased him, "Be patient with God. And don't forget me, ever." And he got that look on his face of amusement, wonder, and intense love that was so essentially himself, and which I will carry with me for the rest of my life.

With his death, his mantle settled down. And though a few days passed before I began to be able to express it, I took that mantle, lashed the water, and called on his God. As prepared as I was for his death, there was no way, in the end, to prepare for it.

There were other losses during the two-week period after his death. My flaky aunt died. With her died a parenting of the free spirit in me. With her death I was kicked out of the nest to free-fall.

She broke away from a stuffy midwestern family way back in the early days of Hollywood, and worked for Central Casting for forty years. It made its mark: she was a combination of Hermione Gingold and Jean Stapleton as Mrs. Archie Bunker. And though for some reason I never really got to know her until about ten years before her death, when we were at my grandfather's funeral, she reinforced, encouraged, and fostered in me against all family pressure the deep knowledge that happiness and holiness do not necessarily come with wealth and power.

Now it is my turn to do the fostering. And while one is nurtured by nurturing, it is never quite the same.

During this same two-week period, a very close friend of mine, another Franciscan, was ordained and celebrated his first Mass. When he crossed into the mystery of his first Consecration, I had an ineffable sense of loss as he began the great and lonely journey which is to be a priest of God. His hands shook as he picked up the chalice, and I felt all of our hearts and invisible hands leap out to steady his—holding up his arms like Moses'—and, sure enough, his hands steadied. But something in his relationship with all of us had quietly, inexorably changed. And no matter how good, how beautiful, and how holy that growth is, there is loss. And we have to let him go.

In that same time-frame I also had to come to terms with the fact that my relationship with some monks to whom I had gone for counsel was also reversing, and because their need was so great, I would no longer be able to lay all my problems and fears and hopes into their kindly hands.

This realization impressed on me the reality of role reversals in virtually every relationship as I grow older, and that from this point on, I would be increasingly and continually asked to change roles. Recently a friend reminded me yet again: *you* are now the older generation. I protest like Jeremiah that I am but a child.

In addition to all this, the usual flux at the friary: people going away to begin new work; people coming home having ended work.

Growing up is hard.

Finally I was able to do a lot of weeping. I did most of it in my sleep. In fact, I went to bed for three days, getting up for offices, Mass, and an occasional meal. A wise man had taught me to grieve that way some years previously.

But this time, it was different. This time instead of using a mere psychological tool, I claimed my sonship in and with Christ, and, crying, "Abba, Father," crawled under the shadow of that Wing we pray about every night at Compline, the image of our Lord's sheltering of us that constantly appears and reappears in the Gospels and the psalms.

I crawled under the shadow of that Wing and slept, and wept, and with that blessed grieving time, the three mornings' long vigils, and a letter from a brother who had been with my Franciscan father during his last moments and at the funeral, the uncontrolled sobbing I needed so badly to release was released. God purified me with grief, and I did a lot of growing up.

I know now the only way to cope with growing up is to become like a little child: to evolve with all our complexity to simplicity; to accept and to trust as a little child trusts, only now with the reconstituted innocence born of sin and pain redeemed that is more precious than the first innocence, and which enables us to walk into the dark closet knowing we will be clobbered, but walking in, trusting, anyway. To love wholeheartedly with wonder and astonishment and delight; to not be afraid of that self-forgetful child's absorption in life, approached uncritically and with suspended judgment.

Grief is indispensable. Jesus knew that. He wept often. He wept at the news of John's death; he wept over Lazarus and the blindness of our hearts; he wept over Jerusalem. Grief made him grow.

And us. It's really the only emotion we have that is un-mixed in content and motive. It purifies our hearts.

Growing up is hard. But we learn. We learn the nuances of life. We learn the difference, for instance, between depression and desolation.

Depression seems always to have an element of unresolved anger and rebellion in it; desolation is like a forest after a fire has gone through: grief has burnt all the anger out, and there is an element of harsh beauty, joy, and even music at the base.

Depression involutes; desolation evolutes. The source of de-pression is often vague; the source of desolation is always specif-ic, for example, it can come not only with a deeper acceptance of one's own solitude, but also after God comes, kindles us into flame, and seems to hide himself again. Depression has no peace and gives no peace; at the bottom of the desolation of the desert is the Peace that passes understanding, the "strife closed in the sod."

Loss of good people, relationships, options, things are worth the grieving. Like Elisha, we lash the water, and it is not only the Jordan that parts for us to cross dry-shod to the prom-ised land; it is a river, too, of tears.

So let us pray for ourselves and our childhood as we pray for those who have died, who precede us to that place where there is no more pain or grief, and where every tear is wiped away from every eye.

May we rest in peace.

Alleluia.

Give rest, O Christ, to your servants, with your saints where sorrow and pain are no more, neither sighing, but life ever-lasting.

You only are immortal, the Creator and Maker of mankind; and we are mortal, formed of the earth, and to earth shall we return. For so you did ordain when you created me, saying,

"You are dust, and to dust you shall return." All of us go down to the dust; yet even at the grave we make our song: Alleluia, alleluia, alleluia.

Give rest, O Christ, to your servants, with your saints where sorrow and pain are no more, neither sighing, but life everlasting.

DECEMBER

◆

Solitude

Solitude

Our culture shrinks from solitude. The cults of narcissism (which is the opposite of solitude) and togetherness whisper insidiously that there is something sick about being solitary—which is very different from being alone.

We are all solitaries.

One measure of the distance at which most people hold solitude is the most frequent comment people make on meeting me: "You don't *look* like a hermit," followed by the query, "What do you *do* in solitude?"

Often I wonder if I'm supposed to have green hair or something, and I'm tempted to reply, "I don't do. I *be*." But in any event, we always seem to end up laughing.

Perhaps there are two questions that underlie this question: Why are people drawn to explore solitude? What is solitude like?

Basically these are unanswerable questions. Each person must try to fathom the answers in the depth of his own heart, beyond words, images, symbols, analogies. Thomas Merton once wrote that all there is to be said about solitude has been said by the wind in the pine trees.

It's helpful to make some distinctions. There is exterior solitude. There is interior solitude. There is interior silence.

You can have exterior solitude and not be in solitude at all because you have a cocktail party or a disco going on in your head.

On the other hand, I've had some very solitary moments on the West Side IRT in Manhattan at rush hour.

And interior silence has very little, if anything, to do with whether or not you are talking to people.

135

One way to answer the first question as to why people are drawn to explore solitude is to look at Jesus and John. They went into hiding in order to come out of hiding, to become bare, exposed, vulnerable, revealed.

Just as surely as John was overjoyed at the appearance of Jesus, when these two towering solitudes met by the bank of the River Jordan, so Jesus recognized that John had the authority of having been in the wilderness where he, Jesus, was going. Jesus came to John as an authority, yet John tried to yield to Jesus.

We know why Jesus went into the wilderness: he was led by the Spirit to be tempted by the devil. You can't separate his baptism from his temptation. He was purified, tempted; God spoke to his heart, and angels came and ministered to him.

But we are told nothing about John from the time of his first recognition of Jesus in his mother's womb until his emergence from the desert to point to the Light himself, who was revealing himself as the Word Incarnate.

John went into the desert to become empty so he could be filled with and sent by God, to point to the light of God. The Evangelist says, ". . . he was not the light but was sent to bear witness to the light, that all men might believe through him."

Jesus, after John's death, refers to him as a lamp. A lamp is filled with light, and the oil that fires the lamp is the oil of repentance. John preached repentance and baptized.

Why?

We have all experienced love as having an unbearable quality to it. John must have experienced this in solitude and baptized to make the One who was coming, Love Incarnate, a little easier to bear. Our baptism in the crucified and risen Christ enables us to bear it; we learn to bear each other's love so we can learn to bear God's.

We are so often like the little kid in the grocery store having a tantrum with his mother's arm around him, loving him at his worst.

And if we remember our own tantrums in our mother's or father's arms, we remember the rage, not only the anger at being thwarted, but also the even greater rage at being loved all the same. It is the hardest thing in the world for that little kid to pass through the terrible loneliness from rage, to the grief that burns the anger out of us so that we can accept our parent's love. Or God's.

George Balanchine's ballet *Prodigal Son* illustrates this passage in a way that leaves you hollow and exhausted. In the beginning the son expresses the aggression of youth, his rage and frustration, by turning away from his home and, crouching like an animal ready to spring, pounding on his knee with both fists.

When the father tries to include him in the family blessing, he pulls away. The father insists; but the moment his back is turned the son repeats the gesture, exploding into the unbelievable leap that has become Villela's and Barishnikov's trademark. The ballet progresses to the son's downfall and abandonment, and we find him totally alone. His loneliness is unbearable. Even more unbearable than love. And then we see the transition to grief, which sets him on the way home to his father's arms.

The wrath of God is his relentless compassion, pursuing us even when we are at our worst.

Lord, give us mercy to bear your mercy.

There is much of this in solitude—yours and mine—this becoming aware of the security blanket of sins whose roots are as unfathomable as they are unspeakable. Having tantrums when this security blanket is taken away. And beginning, again and again, to turn to the unbearable love of God.

And it is always a beginning. Everything becomes a continual beginning.

Beginning to understand what loneliness really is: hunger for God.

We try to fill up that ghastly hole in the pit of our stomachs that is really in our souls. We try to fill it with food, with power, with sex. And there is no more isolating loneliness than that experienced in the most intimate act between two people.

We begin to realize that this hunger will never be satisfied, not in this life. It is the hunger to see God himself, and the only way to approach that is prayer, the prayer that is all of our lives, to yield to his emptiness, his vastness, to lose control of our ideas of him, our ideas and stereotypes of our selves, of our ideas of prayer. We finally—again and again—let go all our concepts of him and begin to understand his concept of us.

At this point I always want to turn and run. It is a little like committing yourself to a river.

At one point in my life I did a lot of whitewater canoeing. You use a canoe without a keel to avoid scraping rocks near the surface. You have a paddle, your instincts, and maybe some rocks in the bow for ballast.

Maybe the rocks in our heads are ballast for the spiritual life.

You learn to read the water, so that after you have passed through a tranquil stretch and come to the rapids, you take what seems the most dangerous path: down the dark V of current to the boiling, violent haystacks of white water which are, in fact, the smoothest way to the calm at the bottom. You try to go into the rapid more slowly than the current so that, at least in the beginning, you have a little control.

But then, as you float down, your heart lurching visibly in your body, you realize that you have passed a point of no return: you are committed. And there is nothing much you can do except trust your skill, your reactions and your boat, to try to avoid the rocks and treacherous eddies marked by smoother, more inviting water, and the great holes, the vortexes, which can swallow a canoe forever.

The river can kill you.

So can God.

But the difference is that in solitude you begin to learn that even if you do plunge into one of those seemingly bottomless holes you are cradled in the hollow of his hand. You are borne by him.

But solitude isn't all, or even frequently, terror.

Sometimes I feel like a little child happily rummaging in an eschatalogical toybox: the toys are icons and the play is for keeps. One of the toys in this box is a theological erector set. It isn't safe to hang anything on the models I build with it, but they catch light refractions from the mirror of the soul.

Sometimes solitude is like balancing on the edge of a razor blade, with a meadow full of wildflowers on one hand, and madness on the other.

Or, solitude is like a tea ceremony, the celebration of life in all its homely movements taken out of time. The wonder of the commonplace; the mystery of ordinary life: eating, sleeping, reading, listening to God's secrets and jokes, a sense of delight, of dance, of coming to fruition, learning that solitude is not something we need to scramble to fill up, but that it is full and overflowing if we can learn to accept the familiarity of insecurity and let go.

Solitude is being poured-out-through.

We evolve toward simplicity. We dwell in the Word.

After all, solitude *is* ordinary life, normal life, though my ordinary is not your ordinary. On one of the standardized IQ tests two definitions of the word "normal" are given: one is "according to a universal standard." The better definition is, "true to type." When we are being normal we are being true to our own type, our own ordinary, our own solitude, our own unique vocation.

Someone wrote me recently and asked if it wasn't frustrating to have exterior solitude interrupted. Well, you learn to live out of your interior solitude. And perhaps this is one of the keys to living in the madness, the telescoping demands and resulting exhaustion of our society: to explore our own interior solitude and learn not only not to be afraid of it but to live out of its self-discipline, its limitless resources and deep Silence.

For me, the normal expression of this is living in a hermitage. For most people, it means something entirely different. For me it means external solitude most of the time; for others, and me sometimes, it means our own interior solitude expressed in ordinary exterior community—family life and work, not just religious community. Holiness is the sanctification of ordinary life.

Self-discipline in this context is the opposite of self-control. When we each find our own ordinary, our vocation, self-discipline helps us break through our psychological crud into a spacious place, into healing and wholeness. It is the struggle to let go, the struggle to open a clenched fist.

Self-control, on the other hand, fighting to force yourself into something that for you is not ordinary, not your vocation, is an ego exercise of domination, a destructive screwing down of the lid.

So, if we are living out of the resources of our solitude in whatever kind of community, we begin to come to realize that we love one another not merely for natural reasons but because each of us has the same love for God, the same hungering for him. We become aware of our brothers' and sisters' holiness and potential holiness, holiness they don't even know about.

And we become aware of their hurts. And our share in these hurts.

We, like John the Baptist, are lamps, our light leaping to-ward each other across the darkness.

This is the role of transparency, that in living out of our own solitude we bear our Lord to one another. Many people came to believe in Jesus through John. We think of this event, of these other events, in what we call history. We think of proph-ets, like mediums, foretelling the future in time.

They aren't. And there isn't.

A few years ago the God is Dead controversy laid to rest, among other things, the concept of the three-storey universe: hell down there, earth in the middle, and heaven up above. We are now struggling to lay to rest the linear concept of time: past, present, future.

Events only seem sequential, physicists tell us. Space and time are one. A particle, the stuff of matter, is not something that can be trapped, but an event in the cosmic dance that can only be observed or even by observation itself participated in. A particle can move up or down, forward or backward, in two di-rections or more at once in space-time.

These physicists tell us that even our concepts of up and down, forward or backward are wrong, that, as Fritjof Capra says in *The Tao of Physics*, ". . . talking about an experience of timeless present is almost impossible because all words like 'timeless,' 'present,' 'past,' 'moment,' refer to the conventional notions of time."

Events only seem sequential. Our concept of time is a convenience, nothing more. We wrestle with the first and second comings, but they are one. It is the Yahweh of the burning bush who is born in the straw and does not consume. The apocalypse began with creation. We say: "Maranatha, come quickly, Lord Jesus." But he is here now.

The prophets and apostles knew this and struggled to break free in their use of language. Isaiah proclaims: "Thus says the Lord, 'Behold I create new heavens and a new earth; and the former things shall not be remembered or come into mind. But be glad and rejoice forever in that which I create; for behold I create Jerusalem a rejoicing and her people a joy.' "

And the Letter to the Ephesians: "In Christ he chose us before the world was founded. . . . He has made known to us his hidden purpose—such was his will and pleasure determined beforehand in Christ—to be put into effect when the time was ripe: namely that the universe, all in heaven and on earth, might be brought into a unity in Christ."

Release from our concepts of time thus enables us to break outside perspective in our solitude. It is in solitude and silence we hear and utter the ineffable Name of the One who uttered himself: God is, therefore, I AM. The Word and the Name are one. And we can neither hear nor speak with words at all, just as Jesus had to use parables to describe the Kingdom of God, just as the liturgy of the Eucharist is a kind of cosmic shorthand, just as these words are foolishness.

When we hear him, when we utter him in the silence of adoration, we participate in creation and the healing and transfiguration of creation. We utter him as we bear him, as our prayer becomes increasingly wordless and imageless; as we participate more deeply in his love we know that the Kingdom of God truly is within us, that we, like John, are bearers of the light, lamps in the windows of God's house, fired with the oil of repentance, keeping us burning with him as we wait for him.

Jesus, Son of the living God, be borne in us today.

There is only one way to answer the questions at the beginning of this essay: you go into the wilderness to be enabled to bear the Word, as the Holy Spirit enabled the prophets to bear it; overshadowed Mary that she might bear him; descended on Jesus empowering him to reveal, to bare, himself as Word made flesh; and at Pentecost gave the disciples what we commonly call the gifts of the Spirit that the Church might bear him, too.

That is all these gifts are: tools to enable us to bear and bare the Word.

We are all solitaries.

No one can take you into the desert. You must find the path yourself. Plunge into your loneliness, your hunger, your thirst. In the desert you will be purified and tempted; God will speak to your heart and angels will come and minister to you.

Out of your own solitude like the prophets you speak the Word; like Mary Theotokos, the God-bearer, you bear and bare him to the world.

Almighty and ever-living God, by your Holy Spirit in the burning bush, in chariots of fire, and in tongues of flame, you have made your people partakers in the radiance of your transfigured Son; strengthen the hearts of your servants: give us courage in temptation and comfort in desolation; show us your paths in the desert that we may find streams of living water; make us holocaust for your people, pure channels of your love, and receive us into the fire of your life, O Blessed Trinity, Father, Son and Holy Spirit, who live and reign in glory everlasting.